HOW TO STUDY
MAGIC

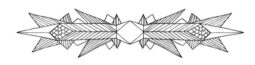

HOW TO STUDY
MAGIC

A GUIDE TO HISTORY, LORE, AND BUILDING YOUR OWN PRACTICE

SARAH LYONS

ILLUSTRATED BY **TOBIAS GÖBEL**

Running Press

PHILADELPHIA

Running Press
Hachette Book Group
1290 Avenue of the Americas, New York, NY 10104
www.runningpress.com
@Running_Press

Printed in Italy

First Edition: October 2022

Published by Running Press, an imprint of Perseus Books, LLC, a subsidiary of Hachette Book Group, Inc. The Running Press name and logo are trademarks of the Hachette Book Group.

The Hachette Speakers Bureau provides a wide range of authors for speaking events. To find out more, go to www.hachettespeakersbureau.com or call (866) 376-6591.

The publisher is not responsible for websites (or their content) that are not owned by the publisher.

Print book cover and interior design by Susan Van Horn.

Library of Congress Control Number: 2022935275

ISBNs: 978-0-7624-7920-7 (hardcover), 978-0-7624-7921-4 (ebook)

Elco

10 9 8 7 6 5 4 3 2 1

CONTENTS

INTRODUCTION

I REMEMBER SO CLEARLY THE DAY I FIRST LEARNED MAGIC WAS REAL.

I was being driven home by my parents when an NPR story on witches in America came on the radio. They talked about something called "Wicca" and people who cast spells and worshipped ancient gods. As someone who had always wished those things were real but was told they weren't, I could hardly believe what I was hearing.

As soon as we got home, I ran up to our family's computer (this was back in the days when you only had one, if any at all), got online, and began to google everything I could about Wicca, witchcraft, and magic.

It's now more than a decade later and I haven't stopped searching and studying, but I have learned a thing or two. I've also had the privilege to watch the magical world change—first from afar, then in the thick of it—over the last several years. How I studied magic when I was younger isn't how people study it today, and in a lot of ways I'm jealous of the wealth of information young witches now have.

However, even with all this information in our pockets, I don't think studying magic has become any less confusing. In fact, in some ways it has become even more so. So many videos, tiktoks, blog posts, books, articles, and tweets get made every second that it can be overwhelming for newcomers and difficult to parse out the good information from the not so good.

Occult means "hidden," and while nothing seems to be hidden these days, the occult has managed to stay a hard topic to grasp. I've seen a lot of magical novices either get so overwhelmed that they back away entirely or get side-tracked down a path that maybe isn't right for them. While your studies of magic and the occult are never really done, I just don't think it has to be so difficult to start.

The idea for this book came when I was trying to answer the question I probably get asked the most: "How do you start doing this stuff?" It's a question that makes me mad—like, get out of my seat, rip off my microphone, and walk off the stage mad. But it's not because it's a bad question, but instead a very good one that doesn't really have an answer. What am I supposed to say? "Go read about ten thousand books, do some psychedelics, and maybe live in the woods for a few years?" That doesn't seem like a satisfying or practical answer for most people. There are so many amazing resources out there on magic, and some great introductory books on specific paths and ideas, but there are very few good books for beginners that look at magic as a whole, because magic is such an individual undertaking.

There's no one way to practice magic, but there are better and worse ways to study it. Basic knowledge of history and context goes a long way in helping you decode the teachings of others as you decide what you want your own practice to look like. I like to think of magic as a way of actively engaging in conversation with the spiritual reality of the cosmos, but it's hard to have a conversation

when you can't speak the language. Basically, I want this book to help you understand what the hell you're looking at next time you walk into an occult bookstore.

This isn't like most books on magic, and it isn't like most books on history either. Part of practicing magic is knowing what you're doing and

why you're doing it, and part of knowing what you're doing is actually practicing it. You (perhaps ironically considering the book in your hands) can't study
magic by just reading—you have to try things out. That's why each of the main
chapters in this book ends with an activity to try and journal prompts to help
you reflect on the things you've just learned. It's also why we'll go over some
basic magical techniques before we get into the main sections on the different
branches of magic. I want this to be a book you can actively engage with, because
that's how magic is best learned.

   We're living in a very strange time, one in which we're awash in a sea
of information, but often have been given very poor tools to navigate it and
weather the occasional storm. This won't be the last book on magic you read—
and it might not even be your first—but if you are new to this world, my hope is
that this book provides you a compass to use as you find your way.

CHAPTER

1

WHY STUDY MAGIC?

So why do you want to study magic anyway?

This might seem like an obvious question, but in my opinion it's a very important one to ask yourself, not just once, but fairly often, as a way to check in with yourself. It's a question I'll bring up again and again as we go through this book. Why study magic? What do you want to get out of a magical practice? What is your life lacking right now that you think magic can give you?

The reason these questions are important is because they will help clarify what you should study and concentrate on. If you need a job fast or have a landlord you need to placate, witchcraft might be a better fit than ceremonial magic. On the other hand, if you are looking for a deep, spiritual, devotional practice, practical spells might not leave you satisfied.

It's also likely that your answer to this question will change over time. When I was a kid, I wanted to do magic because I wanted to gain control over my life, but as I studied and grew, I realized I also wanted a way to understand the world and an ideology that could help me navigate through life.

It's also very possible that you don't know the answer to this question yet. Maybe you just feel a calling to magic. That's great too! Maybe this is the witch in me speaking, but I think of magic as the weeds poking through modernity's concrete. We can try to pave over this disorderly stuff as much as we want, but it will keep popping up—and you might be one of the places it's coming through.

Another question I get asked a lot (almost as much as "how do I study this stuff?") is, "why is magic so popular now?" Usually, I get the feeling that people want me to give them some answer about how magic is a reaction to a world we don't understand or have control over and that in times of crisis people are drawn to magic. There's an argument to be made there, I suppose, but in this question I also sense an underlying assumption that sees magic as *only* a societal reaction, merely a fantasy that emerges when things get dark. Perhaps we should tell the people who built the pyramids or discovered gravity that they didn't understand anything about the world either and were just reacting to chaos. The truth is, magic is about knowing that reality is a two-way street, and I wouldn't always call that a comforting, or reactionary, thought.

Magic can be a lot of things all at once: It's a tool for making your reality a little bit better. It's a philosophy for understanding the world we live in. It's a language through which we can talk to the divine. And it's a technology for self-transformation and betterment. At different points in your magical practice, you will find that different aspects of magic resonate with you. Right now—and maybe this can be our first lesson—I want you to trust your intuition. There can be so much pressure to do and learn everything at once when it comes to magic. I want you to take a breath and slow down before you give in to that imagined pressure. There's probably a feeling or two that guided you this far, and I think you can let that take you through this book. Trust that you have every right and reason to want to study magic. Trust yourself.

And, not that this should really matter, but if someone does try to make you feel like magic is purely the domain of preteens and charlatans, remind yourself that "important" people like Sir Isaac Newton, Sir Arthur Conan Doyle, and W. B. Yeats all practiced magic. The first woman to run for president in the United States, Victoria Woodhull, was a spiritualist and believed she could talk to the dead. The Haitian Revolution—the first successful rebellion of enslaved people of the modern age—was born out of Voodoo and ancient African religions that refused both death and shackles. Magic is very important, and you are not alone in thinking that it is.

PATHS COVERED IN THIS BOOK

Magic is, to put it lightly, a broad topic, and a proper history of magic would take you from the Neolithic period right up through Victorian séances. Since this isn't just a history book, though, we're going to concentrate on five of the most commonly followed paths in modern magic. I'm calling them *paths* and not religions or philosophies because I think it describes the feeling of being a student more accurately. You aren't signing up for a lifelong commitment or getting on a plane to a faraway place, at least not yet. In the beginning, you're traveling down a path, seeing what you find, and deciding whether you want to keep going or not.

The paths that we'll look at in this book are the ones you're most likely to encounter when you start studying magic. They're the ones major occult publishers produce books about, the ones that get shout-outs in the occasional horror movie, and the ones you're most likely to come across in some form if you type *magic* into a search engine. While this list is not exhaustive, I think that having a grasp of all these paths will serve you well as you study magic, even if you decide none of them are quite for you.

The paths are:

◆ CHAOS MAGIC

If you like the idea of forging your own path, if you hate your reality being dictated by others, and if you like the idea of your spirituality being defined as "fuck around and find out," then you will like chaos magic. A postmodern form of magic, chaos magic is the youngest path in this book. It holds that reality is a construction that you can define for yourself and that "nothing is true, everything is permitted."

◆ WITCHCRAFT

If you picked up this book, there's a good chance you are interested in witchcraft. Possibly the most popular form of magic today, *witchcraft* is a broad term that encompasses folk beliefs, herbal wisdom, neopagan goddess worship, and land-based practical magic, depending on whom you ask. If anything I just mentioned sounds appealing to you, you should check out witchcraft.

◆ GRIMOIRES

If you were inspired to get into magic because of horror movies that feature ancient spell books, or if your idea of a good time is spending all day in the library, you might be drawn to grimoire magic. Grimoires are the ancient spell books of Europe and the Middle East and the magic contained within them. Demons, angels, gods, and the planets and how to speak to them are all found here.

◆ CEREMONIAL MAGIC

If you are someone who likes to rise to a challenge, who thrives with clear goals and degrees of progress, and who likes the idea of inner discipline as a core of your spiritual practice, then ceremonial magic might be for you. Developed in the Middle Ages and popularized in the nineteenth century, this form of magic places great emphasis on learning, ritual, and progressing through spiritual degrees.

◆ PAGANISM

If you are less drawn to practical magic and more drawn to the idea of religion, or if you are more interested in simply communing with gods and spirits than making them work for you through spells, paganism might be worth looking into. A broad term for pre-Christian spirituality, paganism has grown steadily more popular in the last half century.

PATHS NOT COVERED IN THIS BOOK

There are more magical paths outside of this book than inside of this book. The reason I'm not covering them all is 1) word count, and 2) I'm just not an expert in a lot of these paths. I haven't practiced them, and I don't feel I am the right person to give you an introduction to them.

Specifically, I'm talking about African Diasporic Religions, or ADR. These are religions and forms of magic that were carried by enslaved people from Africa to the Americas and Caribbean during the slave trade. Things like Voodoo, Santeria, Palo, Quimbanda, Umbanda, and many others all fall under this umbrella. Most of these paths require some form of initiation for the practitioner to be considered part of the religion (more on initiation later), and all of them have very complex worldviews and histories that I simply am not an expert on.

If you are interested in following any of these paths, I recommend reading books and blogs by people who are part of the religions and, if you can, learning directly from these teachers. I'll put some recommended reading on this in the final chapter, in case you would like to delve into these traditions.

If in the course of your magical studies you find a practice, path, or form of magic that appeals to you but that I don't talk about here, my hope is that this book will give you the foundation and tools to explore more.

HOW TO USE THIS BOOK

I'm going to assume that if you picked up this book, you are already studying magic in some way. You might have a hundred browser tabs open right now, a pile of books by your bed, or a thousand videos saved to watch later (all of which you'll get around to at some point . . . right?).

While I was writing this book, I tried to put myself back into the mindset of a beginner and think about what would have been useful to me when I was starting out.

Basically, what I discovered with this process is that what I think I longed for more than anything in the early days of my studies was a friend. I wish I had someone to ask questions of, who could be there to see if what I was doing was "right." I got so many false starts and went down so many rabbit holes thinking "this is absolutely the bestest, most correct form of magic," only to discover later that things are much more complicated than they seemed. In the long run, I think it worked out okay for me. I learned a lot walking down endless "wrong" paths, and I'm lucky to now have a magical community around me where I can compare notes. But I still can't help but wonder where I'd be if I had had a book like this one at the beginning.

With that in mind, there are a few different ways to use this book.

Your first option is to read it cover to cover, like any normal book. After the chaos magic chapter, the book will proceed more or less chronologically—if that helps you learn and put things into context, then that could be the right way for you to approach it. You might also have picked this book up to learn about one of the specific paths covered—in which case, you can head right to that chapter first. You might also want to use this book as a reference tool to pop open when you encounter something you don't understand in your broader studies.

The difference between this book and similar encyclopedias, references, and history books is that you can work *with* this book. In the next chapter we'll go over some basic magical ideas and "tech" that you can apply to any of the paths described here. Come across an idea you like or a thing you want to try out? This book will help you do that. It's my personal belief that magic can't just be read about. In order to be understood, it has to be tried out. So, as with a good cookbook, I want you to read, tinker, and get creative with this book.

CHAPTER

2
THE BASICS

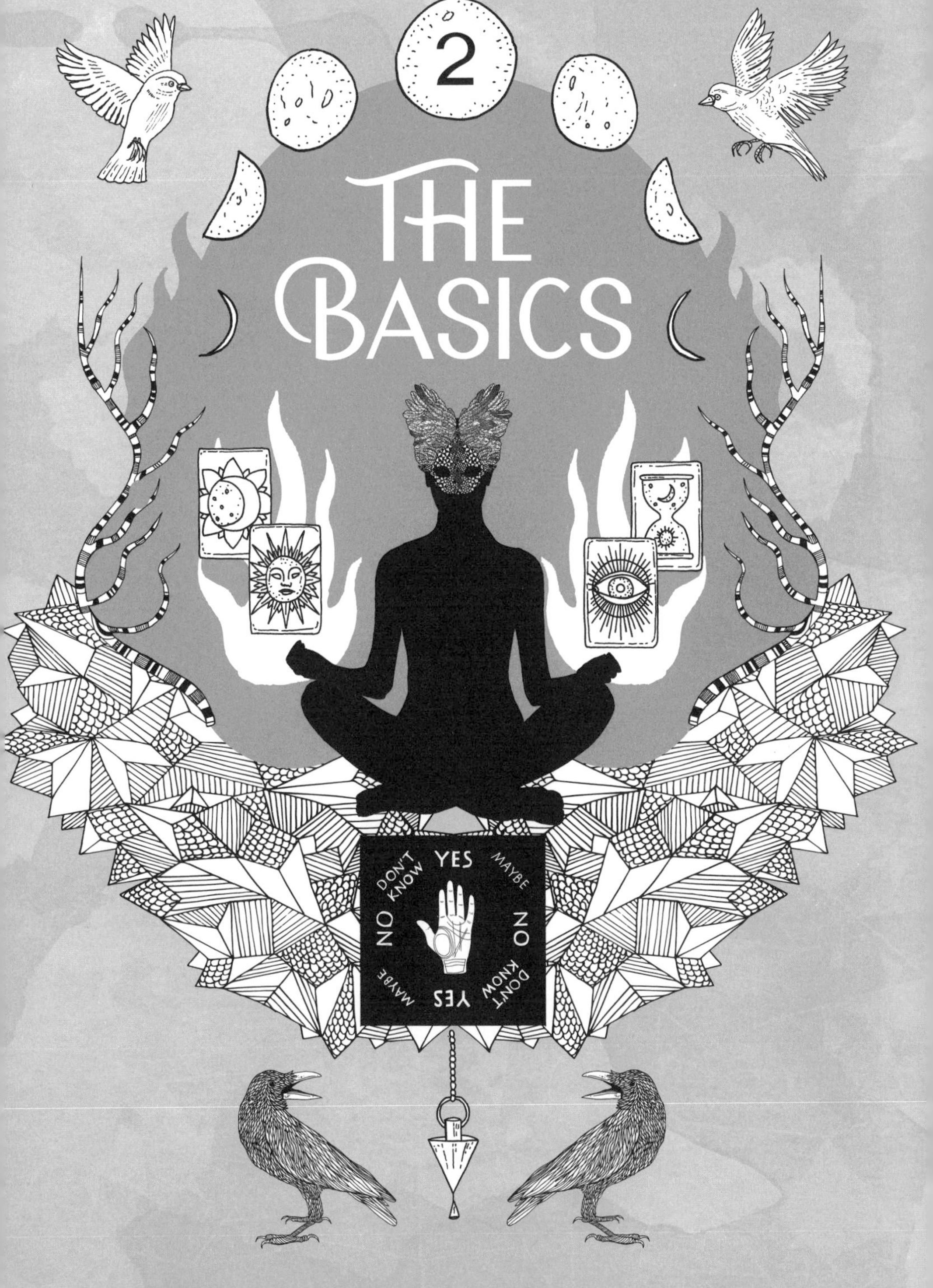
YES
MAYBE
NO
DON'T KNOW
YES
MAYBE
NO
DON'T KNOW

S omething I will emphasize over and over again is that there are many ways to study, practice, and enter into magic, and no one way is the "correct" one. With that in mind, I do think there are some basic skills and tools you should have in your kit, so to speak, before you start trying other things out. Think of it this way: I don't really think there's a "right" way to have sex for the first time, but I do think there are a couple wrong ways to do it—mostly because you could end up hurting someone or being hurt yourself. Knowing how to protect yourself, what your body needs, and how to communicate with others will go a long way not just in the beginning, but throughout your life. And magic is no exception.

In this chapter, I'm going to walk you through some basic magical tech that you'll need as you navigate the paths in this book. All of these things could, and do, have books of their own. They can also be found in most, if not all, spiritual and magical traditions, and because of that, they each have many different styles and techniques. As your own practices grow and deepen, you will probably refine what you find here to meet your own needs, and that's a good thing! For now, we are going to keep it really simple.

DIVINATION

How do you talk to a god? How do you make sure the information you are getting from a spirit is truthful? How do you know which offerings to leave, which books to buy, or which tree to meditate at? When in doubt, I find the answer is usually divination.

Most people think of divination as simply a way to predict the future. Tarot cards, pendulums, runes, and scrying are some of the most popular and well-known methods of divination. While it's true that all of these can be used to make predictions about the future, they can also be employed for much more.

Divination is an excellent way to check in on magical experiences you will have, especially if you don't have a magical community or people in your life to turn to when you have questions. Let's say you find a particularly beautiful rock at a place that's sacred to you. You get a feeling that you're supposed to use this somehow, but you don't know how, or if it's even a good idea to take this rock in the first place. Divination can be an excellent way to clarify all this.

There is no one best divination technique to learn. Some, in my opinion, are better suited to certain types of questions than others. But as with everything in this book, you can only gain an understanding of what works best for you by practicing and paying attention.

On the following pages you'll find some divination tools that are fairly common and easy to use. We don't have the space to go into each one in too much depth, but at the end of this chapter you can find a list of books that contains excellent resources for learning more.

PLAYING CARDS

People are often shocked when I tell them playing cards can be used in magic, as though they expect that something so common can't possibly be magical! The truth is, many household items have been used in folk magic for centuries, and playing cards are no exception.

While playing cards can be used to answer pretty much any question you like, I think they are an especially great way of asking simple yes-or-no questions.

To perform this type of divination, shuffle your deck as you ask your question out loud. When you are ready, draw three cards. Red means "yes" and black means "no."

Three red cards = a definitive yes

Two red cards = a qualified yes

Two black cards = a qualified no

Three black cards = a definitive no

Like tarot cards, playing cards each have their own unique meanings and interpretations. Knowing this context can give you more insight into the yeses and noes you receive in answer to your questions. For instance, if you pull three black cards and one is the Four of Spades, the particular message of this card is you might get sick if you attempt the thing you're asking about.

As simple or as complicated as you want to make them, playing cards are an excellent divination tool to take up in your magical practice.

PENDULUMS

Pendulums are easy and versatile tools for spirit communication and divination. Usually, pendulums are comprised of a stone or piece of metal hung from a single chain so that it can swing freely, but necklaces and even extremely decorative pieces can serve as pendulums as well.

To use a pendulum, you can either hold the end of the string in your hand, or tie it to a hook or fixed object so that it can swing freely from there. While pendulums are not great for answering complex questions, they can respond to yes or no questions in several different ways. Try the different methods out, and see which ones work best for you.

- Hold the pendulum between your thumb and forefinger, and ask your questions. If it spins counterclockwise, your answer is no, and if it spins clockwise, your answer is yes.

- Similarly, hold the pendulum and ask your question. Swinging perpendicularly to your body means "yes" and swinging parallel to your body means "no."

- As with ouija boards, you can use a physical chart to help with pendulum divination. While there are plenty of boards you can buy, to make your own simple pendulum

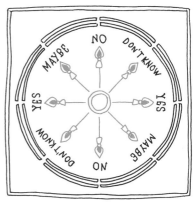

chart, draw the image here on a piece of paper. Where the pendulum swings is your answer.

◆ If you are trying to communicate with a specific place or object, you can hold your pendulum over the object as you ask your questions. You can also use a photo of a loved one who has passed away, the image of a deity, or a map for a similar effect.

I'll be honest: pendulums aren't really my thing. I can never seem to get out of my head when I'm using them, so I always worry that I'm the one moving them. It's important to take things like this into account when you're building your practice. If something works for you, keep doing it. If something doesn't work or just doesn't sit right, don't be afraid to discard it or change it up a bit.

BOOKS

Bibliomancy, or divination using a book, is very old.

Historically, in both Europe and the Americas, bibliomancy was performed with a copy of the Bible. Today, you might prefer to use other sacred texts or any book with a special significance to you. I have a friend who has several old Bibles and shuffles them before performing divination. For a time, I used a wilderness survival guide as a divination tool. Remember, it's okay for your magic to be silly!

Bibliomancy is easy. Simply pick up your book of choice, ask your question, close your eyes, and flip through the book until you feel the urge to stop. Place your finger on the page, and the passage you have landed on is your answer.

If you are using the Bible, keep in mind that "red letter passages"—passages where Jesus is speaking, which are set in red type in some editions—are considered particularly powerful.

You might choose to keep one or several books for use exclusively in divination. You might choose to use your most worn-out and well-read paperback.

What I like about bibliomancy is that it can be done on the fly when you've left your tarot cards at home or feel weird breaking out a pendulum. Most people won't bat an eye at you flipping through a book in public. All you need for bibliomancy is a clear question, a clear intention, and a book.

TAROT

Probably one of the most popular forms of divination today, tarot is also one of the most rich and complicated.

There's a lot of debate about when tarot was officially created, but it's widely accepted that playing cards and card games first arrived in Southern Europe from the Middle East in the 1300s. Tarot decks, originally adapted from playing cards, are divided into two main sections: the major arcana and the minor arcana, with *arcana* meaning "mystery." The minor arcana corresponds to a standard playing card deck, with four suits (Wands, Cups, Swords, and Pentacles) and fourteen cards in each suit. The major arcana are the named cards that people generally think of when they picture tarot—like Death, the High Priestess, and the Moon. Throughout the Middle Ages, many different regional and artistic variations of tarot were created (in Germany they had Bells and Acorns for suits instead of Swords and Wands), and the deck we have now was only standardized fairly recently.

Even though tarot was first created in the Middle Ages, it wasn't until the nineteenth century that it was revamped and experienced a new wave of popularity—something we'll discuss in more depth in chapter 5. For now, just know that an occultist—the guy who coined that term in fact—named Eliphas Levi synchronized the tarot with something called "Hermetic Qabalah"; and this was later adopted by a group called the Golden Dawn, who also added astrological correspondences to the cards.

You might find these associations and correspondences helpful—or you might not. I personally only consider them when I find it useful, and many people don't take them into account at all. Tarot is a big subject; it's a tool that you can spend a lifetime meditating on and using in many ways.

Because of how complicated tarot is, I personally like to utilize it for big, general questions about my life, rather than questions I'm asking of a specific deity or spirit. If I'm asking a spirit, "Would you like me to bring you white flowers each week?" and I pull the Five of Wands, I don't really know what to do with that. But three red playing cards instead will give me a clear yes.

Now, again, your mileage may vary. Tarot has remained one of the most popular forms of divination for more than a century for good reason, and it has become incredibly popular in the last ten years. Many artists have crafted their own interpretation of the cards and added their own spin on tarot. This means you can use one deck for some problems, and other decks for others. (I personally only break out my Thoth tarot deck when I have a fairly existential question in mind.)

These are just a handful of divination techniques you might explore—and there are many more out there. I chose to highlight these because they are accessible, fairly common, and as such have a lot of resources on them. I recommend giving each a try and seeing what works best for you. It's very likely you'll be drawn to more than one, and over time which one you use will be determined by the question you ask.

As a general way to get started with divination, I like to pick a method, use it every day for at least a week, and see how it works. Ask it a simple question like "How will my day go?" or "What advice should I keep in mind today?" and see how accurate the response is. If a form of divination doesn't work for you or just doesn't feel right, put it aside in favor of one that does.

MEDITATION

I know that meditation might seem boring—or like the magical equivalent of cleaning your room or going to the gym—but it has survived for centuries for a reason. Meditation is how we learn to calm and focus the mind, which is a very important skill to cultivate when doing magic.

In recent years, companies out of Silicon Valley have popularized things like mindfulness meditation—the practice in which you sit still and concentrate on your breath and the current moment—but that is by no means the only method of meditation. In many ways, I think this corporate takeover of meditation has made it very standardized in places like the United States, which often leaves people thinking that meditation is all about sitting uncomfortably, closing your eyes, and focusing on your breathing. While there is absolutely value in mindfulness meditation, meditation as a whole is much broader, and there are many ways to go about it.

We won't examine every meditative technique, but it's important to understand what meditation is and to get a basic grasp of it so you can use it while you study. Daily or routine meditation is a very popular wellness technique with good reason. Previously scoffed at, meditation's mental and physical health benefits have been demonstrated in more and more recent studies. While the health benefits of meditating are a welcome side effect of practicing magic, it's not the only reason to learn how to do it.

In magical lingo, meditation means creating a meaningful shift in consciousness. Perhaps you've felt this while dancing and losing yourself to the rhythm or while driving a familiar route and suddenly arriving at your destination without really remembering how you got there. Anything that lets your conscious brain turn off for a bit is meditative. When we do this intentionally, other worlds, spirits, and inner messages can become available to us.

Speaking personally, almost every piece of intentional magic I do involves meditation on some level. Whether it's a brief quieting of the mind while I leave offerings or taking a deep journey to talk to spirits, meditation plays a role in my practice. And no matter where you are in your studies, meditation of some sort is an invaluable magical skill to learn.

With all that in mind, here are some simple meditation techniques. As with divination, I recommend trying each for just five to ten minutes a day for a week or so and seeing how they feel. You might find that just one technique works well for all your needs, or you might like using a variety, each for a different purpose.

Keep in mind that meditation is way more difficult than it looks. That's not meant to frighten you away from doing it—in fact, recognizing that meditation is hard can be really liberating, because it means you don't need to be perfect. You're absolutely going to have random thoughts pop into your head, and you will likely find it difficult to concentrate at first. Try not to beat yourself up over this; it happens to even the most experienced meditators. Just try your best and keep at it—it really will get easier with practice.

① MINDFULNESS MEDITATION

+ Light a candle or burn some incense if you feel moved to do so. This isn't strictly necessary, but I find it helps a lot of people get into the right head-space for meditation.

+ Sit down with your legs crossed or lie down in a comfortable position—but not one that is so comfortable you will fall asleep. You may sit on a cushion or folded blanket if that is helpful.

+ Take a moment to settle into your body. Stretch if you need to, scratch your nose if you need to, etc.

+ Once you've settled, take one deep breath in through your mouth, totally filling your lungs, hold for four seconds, then exhale again through your mouth until your lungs are completely empty.

+ Begin what is called *box breath* or the *fourfold breath*. This is a technique in which you'll breathe in through your nose for four seconds, hold for four seconds, breath out through your mouth for four seconds, and hold again for four seconds, before repeating.

+ Do this for five to ten minutes, trying to clear your mind and concentrating only on your breathing. If your mind wanders or you catch yourself thinking about something else, simply acknowledge the thought and let it go. Come back to the breathing or the counting.

② WALKING MEDITATION

+ Find a pleasant place to walk where you won't be disturbed. If it's a spot where you won't be observed, that's even better. This can look strange to outsiders, and even if you live in a city where people are generally okay with weirdness, removing the potential for embarrassment or self-consciousness is best for your meditation. Try to find a nature walk, a quiet neighborhood, or even just a room in your home.

+ Take a deep breath in through your nose and out through your mouth.

+ Begin walking at a slow pace, taking ten to fifteen steps in one direction.

+ As you walk, pay attention to your body. How does the earth feel beneath your feet? What about your clothes on your skin? Can you feel your blood flowing, your muscles and bones supporting you? As always, keep your breathing steady.

+ When you come to the end of your steps, take another breath in through your nose and out through your mouth.

+ Turn around and repeat your steps. Do this for five to ten minutes.

While sitting comfortably and breathing might work for some people as an effective way to quiet the mind and enter a sense of mental flow, it doesn't work for everyone. For a lot of people, moving the body is the best way to enter a meditative state. Athletes and dancers often say they reach this state of mind when they are in the middle of a game or routine. If you feel your meditation practice needs more embodiment, try the above method and see how it feels.

③ BEAM OF LIGHT

+ Sit or stand in a quiet place.

+ Take a deep breath in through your nose, filling your lungs completely, then breath out through your mouth, emptying your lungs completely.

+ Begin to breathe steadily, in through your nose and out through your mouth.

+ Imagine a white light climbing up from the earth and flowing into you. The light slowly rises with each breath, traveling up your spine until it reaches your center.

+ Now start to imagine another beam of light coming down from above. The light flows into you through your head, moving down until it meets the other beam of light.

+ As the two light beams meet, they form a ball of light that grows bigger and bigger until it fills your whole being.

+ Once you have felt this light fill you and energize you, begin to return your attention to your physical body and your breath. Slowly bring yourself back to where you are, and when you are ready, open your eyes.

This meditation is helpful for something commonly referred to as energy work. We won't cover that concept much in this book, but this style of meditation can also be helpful for blessings, spell work, or whenever you feel your body needs a bit of a recharge. If you aren't used to visualizing during meditation, a simple one like this can be a good way to get started.

CLEANSING

Cleansing is an important part of spiritual health. Keeping your body and space clean in a spiritual manner is just as important as what you routinely do physically. As you try different paths in this book and build a practice of your own, it's a good idea to engage in regular cleansing.

In some traditions, cleansing is so important it must be engaged with before any magical working can be done. Ceremonial magic, for instance, is big on this.

In others, it is slightly less important, but still something you should do occasionally. Regardless of your path, cleansing is a part of most spiritual traditions, and having a basic grasp of it is a good idea before diving into practicing magic.

While there are many ways to cleanse oneself that are specific to particular regions, religions, and paths, I'm going to cover two very basic and widely accessible forms here.

BURNING

Burning herbs, incense, or resin for cleansing is a very common practice. From the Roman and later Catholic use of frankincense to indigenous South American use of palo santo, burning is a method of cleansing that shows up across cultures and time.

There is a lot of discussion right now about the ethics of burning and using certain plants in magic. White sage, in particular, has become a point of controversy, with many saying that the plant is not only endangered, but that people who are not indigenous to Turtle Island (North America), where the plant is native, shouldn't use it.

While white sage is not currently endangered—you wouldn't be seeing it at major retailers if it were—I do think there are ethical considerations to think about when using this and other plants in your own magical practice. Speaking as a witch and animist for a moment, I want to recognize that plants are not just objects—they are beings with their own stories, personalities, and histories. Reducing a plant down to one quality (e.g., sage = cleansing) is a fairly new and colonial idea, and no matter which plants you are utilizing, I encourage you to get to know them a bit before applying them in magic.

Now, you might feel like it's not a big deal when you use a certain plant or material because "you know what you're doing" or you're using it for the "right" reasons, unlike "those people," and maybe you're right. This isn't a book that will tell you what you absolutely should or should not do. I will invite you, though, to consider how your actions impact others, and what ethical considerations you might need to take in light of that impact. Consider, for example, that it was illegal for Indigenous people to use sage or practice their own ceremonies in the United States for a long time, while white people happily burned away ghosts with sage. Or, if this is a plant that's being overharvested, is it possible to grow your own? If not, can you buy from someone who is growing it or ethically harvesting it themselves? Magic, ideally, deepens your connection to the world around you, so consider the connections you want to foster through your practice.

Below are some herbs commonly burned for cleansing:

◆ Cedar   ◆ Rosemary   ◆ Juniper   ◆ Frankincense

Like I said, I don't like to substitute herbs willy-nilly for things like this, because although all the items above can be used for cleansing, they all have different histories, lore, and uses. They don't always make a good 1:1 ratio. However, if you are just getting started in magic, I would pick a plant or resin from the list above, use it in your practice, and learn what you can about it before moving on to the next one.

As your practice grows and evolves, you'll likely find yourself needing to cleanse your person, your space, or your ritual tools in a different way than I'll lay out here. In the beginning though, use the following systems of cleansing and see how they work.

① Once a week, cleanse your home, room, or the space where you do magical workings. Begin at the back of your house or space and light whichever herbs you want to use. Move counterclockwise through your space with the smoke, paying close attention to doors, windows, and mirrors, and conclude at your front door or the entrance to your space.

② Before and after a ritual, burn your herbs and, using a scooping motion, spread the smoke up over your head, down your arms, and over your body.

③ Before a ritual, use the smoke from your herbs to "wash down" whatever tools you are using.

Because cleansing can feel really good, it's easy to become addicted to it at first. You might find yourself cleansing yourself every day or even several times a day. I think how much you cleanse depends on the type of work you are doing, the environment you live in, and your own personality. I've known people who lived in really dangerous situations, like unsafe households or prison, who cleansed themselves several times a day to keep their environment from spiritually sticking to them. However, if you are doing fairly basic magic and live in a happy environment, you might only need to do this once or twice a week. Just like antibiotics are good, but can strip your gut of healthy bacteria if you aren't careful, overcleansing yourself or your space can make it antiseptic to spirits. Try the above techniques a few times a week at first, and feel out if you need to adjust up or down.

WASHING

Bathing, washing, and water are other ways to cleanse yourself or your space. If you can't burn herbs or resins, using water as a cleansing method can be a great option. There's a long tradition in hoodoo, rootwork, and American folk magic of floor washes and baths that is worth looking into, but for now we are going to keep things simple.

If you are Christian or come from a tradition that uses holy water, you can always use that to cleanse and purify yourself and your space. Most cathedrals give or sell holy water, and you can ask a priest to bless water that you bring him. If you prefer to make your own, however, there are a number of easy options.

If you live near the ocean, or even if you go to the beach once or twice a year for a trip, you can always cleanse yourself by dipping into the sea. Say a prayer on the shore, then walk or dive into the water so you are totally submerged. Seawater can also be used to cleanse your space, but due to the live organisms— and quite frankly the smell—I don't personally recommend this.

The two best types of water to use for cleansing a space are spring and river water. If you live near one or both types of bodies of water, feel free to harvest some for your own use. If, on the other hand, you don't, consider that the water from your tap likely comes from one of these sources and so is just fine for cleansing.

We're living at a time when water is an increasing battleground for human and land rights. Pipelines and factory farms often harm rivers and the people who live near them, and fights over who controls the destiny of water seem to only grow more animated. I would do some research on the water you are using in your rituals and see if there is such a battle happening over it. Consider making donations that help people who are fighting to protect water or giving back in some way to the water that you use.

Once you have your water, there are a few ways to consecrate it for cleansing. The easiest way is to simply pray over it, but if you want to get a little fancy, add salt or hyssop to your water. If you use hyssop to make water for cleansing, consider reciting Psalm 51:7 over the water, as it's the traditional psalm to use for this purpose:

> *Purge me with hyssop, and I shall be clean: wash me,*
> *and I shall be whiter than snow.*

Just like with smoke, you can sprinkle concentrated water around where you do magic, wash yourself or your hands with it, or wash your magical tools with it.

GROUNDING

When you finish with a spell, working, or meditation, it's good to bring yourself back to the present and "ground" back in your body.

You might want to do this for a couple of reasons. The first is that going straight from magical work to the mundane world can be jarring, especially if what you were doing was a bit dark or dramatic. The other reason is safety. You want all parts of you—mind, body, and spirit—to come back together and be in concert, not still lingering on your working well after it's passed. Keep in mind that you don't have to ground after every single bit of magic, but it's good to know how for bigger workings.

You'll find all sorts of rituals and exercises for grounding, and while those might work for some, keeping it simple and a little normie is what helps me calm down and relax.

If you finish doing magic and feel you need to ground back into your body, my first recommendation is to have a drink of water and something simple to eat, like toast or crackers. This will get your metabolism moving and your body working, and it will help you settle back into your home state. If you're still feeling a little unmoored, try watching or reading something that has absolutely nothing to do with the work you just did. Going for a walk with a silly podcast or watching your favorite television show can bring your awareness back to this reality and out of a magical mindset.

KEEPING A MAGICAL JOURNAL

Throughout this chapter, I'm sure you've noticed how much I've encouraged you to try things out on your own to see how they fit into your own practice. This is because magic—especially if you aren't working within a formal system or religion—is often a very personal thing. What works for me might not work for you.

It's important that you try new things, experiment with techniques, and test out spells and workings. We're all different, and over time you'll find that *your* magic works in a way that's special and unique to you, even if only slightly.

To keep track of these things in the early stages of your study, it's a good idea to keep a magical journal. This can be part of the nightly journal you already have as part of a self-care practice, or it can be a journal all its own. I personally can't keep track of too many journals, so I have one nightly diary that

I use and will record special magical occurrences or workings as they come up for me, just like any other event. If you think a separate journal just for magic would be best for you, then this section will help you craft that.

Whether you use it for keeping track of divination that you do, logging what comes up during meditation, or taking notes on what worked or didn't work in a spell, a magical journal can be a great way to figure out what works best for your magical practice.

Some say you must record every single aspect of your day and the conditions you were doing magic under to make a "real" magical journal. What you were wearing, what the weather was like, where you were, the sun signs of the people you did magic with, and so forth, are all things that absolutely must be recorded for future study if you are to be a real magician! Or so some say.

I leave it up to you how detailed you want to be in your recordings. You might find it useful to keep extremely detailed notes, but I personally find this turns magic into a bit of a chore, which frankly takes the magic out of magic for me.

The truth is, there are no set rules for keeping or making a magical journal. The idea is that you are watching out for patterns in your life and then maximizing or ritualizing those patterns to make your magic even stronger. For this reason, there are some natural cycles and things to keep in mind that are good starting points for most people.

For instance, let's say you do a spell that begins on the full moon and ends on the new moon, and it works great! You try a similar one again, and it also works great. But over time you discover that spells you do outside of this cycle aren't as effective. This might tell you to only do big workings between the full and new moon, or that you'll need extra help at other times of the month.

This is just one example, and you may find that other cycles are more relevant for you. To get going, let's look at some magical cycles and correspondences that are worth starting out your journal with.

PLANETARY CORRESPONDENCES

We will go into more detail on the history behind this in chapter 5, but in short, each day of the week corresponds to one of the seven classical planets. The correspondences are:

Monday → Moon

Tuesday → Mars

Wednesday → Mercury

Thursday → Jupiter

Friday → Venus

Saturday → Saturn

Sunday → Sun

In addition to the days of the week, the hours of the day are also ruled by the seven classical planets. There are free apps that track this for you, which I'll list at the end of the chapter, but for now, here is a chart of hourly correspondences. It begins on the first hour of each day (1 a.m.) and cycles from there:

Feel free to copy this chart into the first page of your journal as a helpful tool to check back on.

Since planetary magic is such a big part of Western occultism, I think these correspondences can be useful markers to keep track of. Personally, I often use days of the week to time my magic, but not hours of the day. For me, aligning hours with my practice simply ends up being less a tool of magic, and more a tool of procrastination. See what works for you by keeping track of the day and hour you do magic, see strange things, or wake from dreams.

HOURLY / WEEKLY PLANETARY CHART

HOUR	SUN	MON	TUES	WED	THU	FRI	SAT
1	☉	☽	♂	☿	♃	♀	♄
2	♀	♄	☉	☽	♂	☿	♃
3	☿	♃	♀	♄	☉	☽	♂
4	☽	♂	☿	♃	♀	♄	☉
5	♄	☉	☽	♂	☿	♃	♀
6	♃	♀	♄	☉	☽	♂	☿
7	♂	☿	♃	♀	♄	☉	☽
8	☉	☽	♂	☿	♃	♀	♄
9	♀	♄	☉	☽	♂	☿	♃
10	☿	♃	♀	♄	☉	☽	♂
11	☽	♂	☿	♃	♀	♄	☉
12	♄	☉	☽	♂	☿	♃	♀

LUNAR CYCLES

Another natural cycle I like to keep track of is the lunar cycle. The phases of the moon have measurable effects on tides and large bodies of water, and some believe there is evidence they can affect emotions, menstrual cycles, and even crime rates.

In addition, farming practices have been governed by the moon for centuries. Since the moon rules the tides, the old idea was that it governed the movement of all moisture, making the new moon good for planting and the full moon good for harvesting. Biodynamic farming practices today use the moon and stars to determine the best times to plant and harvest crops.

In Europe, this idea can be traced at least as far back as ancient Rome. In the first century BCE, the Roman naturalist Pliny the Elder wrote in his book *Natural History* that the moon "replenishes the earth; when she approaches it, she fills all bodies, while, when she recedes, she empties them."

This idea has been adopted into a lot of popular folk magic and modern witchcraft traditions. Typically, if you want to cut something out of your life, or diminish something's power, work while the moon is waning. If you want to grow something, or bring something into your life, work while the moon is waxing.

Before we go any further, I want to take a minute to say something. All of these are commonly used tools and ideas that many find helpful in their magic. I present them here because in the beginning of any study, especially that of magic, some sort of structure can be really helpful. However, if this is all overwhelming you and intimidating you from studying magic at all, then it's okay to keep it simple. You are (most likely) not going to accidentally summon YogSothoth if you do your love spell on a Thursday rather than a Friday. I would much rather you dive in and build your practice as you go than think you need to have every planetary hour and color association memorized before you even start. Take what is helpful for you in this section and go from there.

SAMPLE PAGE

Here is an example of what a page in a magical journal could look like. Feel free to copy this format or make something up yourself.

DATE: ☉ Sunday 5/2/21

TIME: ♀ 3:29 p.m.

WEATHER: clear skies, cool

MOON: waning gibbous

SPELL WORK PERFORMED: dreams, synchronicities

THINGS OF NOTE:

ON SYNCHRONICITY

Let's take this opportunity to discuss synchronicity and how it might pop up for you while you study magic.

The word *synchronicity* was coined by ~~occultist~~ psychologist Carl Jung, who described it as a "meaningful coincidence of two or more events where something other than the probability of chance is involved."

A synchronicity is a coincidence that feels like more than a coincidence. There is meaning and strangeness surrounding synchronicity in a way that there isn't around something like you and your friend just wearing the same color shirt one day.

In magic, synchronicities are like markers on a path to show us that we are going in the right direction. If you aren't experiencing synchronicities, that's not necessarily a bad thing, but when you do start to experience them, you should really pay attention.

It's hard to describe the difference between a coincidence and a synchro-nicity with just words, because so much of the difference comes from an inter-nal sense of meaning. Coincidences happen all the time, and it's important to remember that so you don't go looking for syncs where there are none. Reading a popular book in the park and then looking up to see someone else reading that same book might just be a fun coincidence. However, if the idea to read that book came to you in a dream and the other person reading the book has on the same outfit you were wearing in said dream, we're approaching the realm of synchronicity.

Once you learn about synchronicities, it might be tempting to try to find them everywhere. You might squint your eyes, tilt your head, and say, "Well, I read about Diana last night and I saw a picture of a moon today; I guess that could be a sync." Trust me, though: you won't have to force yourself to recognize a synchronicity when it happens. It will feel weird and often follows a dreamlike logic. If I had to describe the feeling, it's like a puzzle piece just clicked into place inside you. It likely won't be weird to anyone else but you, but you will almost certainly feel very weird.

As you study magic, it's likely that synchronicities will happen to you. Pay attention and make note of them when they do, as they are powerful indicators that your magic is working and you are doing what you are supposed to.

Don't worry if synchronicities don't happen right away or if they stop happening for a period of time. The reason these moments are special is because we don't experience them all the time. You shouldn't try to force yourself to see syncs where there are none. It's natural for things to settle down even after a flurry of activity, so while it's a good sign, if a spooky one, when synchronicities start appearing, it's not necessarily a bad sign when they stop. If you are concerned or fear that a disconnect is occurring between you and a deity, spirit, or practice, remember that this is where divination comes in.

FURTHER RESOURCES

A Deck of Spells, Charles Porterfield
There are few books I'll recommend here that I'll describe as indispensable, but this might be one. Short, straightforward, and packed with useful information, this book is the one to get if you want to take up divination with playing cards.

Oak Meditation app
This free app doesn't have the frills or hundreds of guided meditations that other apps do, but that's part of why I like it. Personalize the sounds and length of the meditation you want, and track hours meditated in this simple app.

Spiritual Cleansing, Draja Mickaharic
A classic for a reason, this short but dense book is filled with excellent methods of cleansing that are great for beginners.

Time Nomad Astrology app
There are tons of free astrology apps, and this is just the one I use. Look up charts, check out the current skies, and download the widget that tracks planetary hours.

CHAOS
MAGIC

et's get something cleared up right off the bat: I'm calling it *magic*, not *magik*, *magick*, or *majick*. This book isn't being written in the 1990s.

Now that we have that out of the way, let's introduce chaos magic (and why some people spell it with a *k*).

While the rest of this book is laid out more or less chronologically, we're going to start with the youngest form of magic we'll be looking at. Chaos magic is a postmodern form of magic—with most of its foundational texts having been written in the last few decades and ideas and language that are fairly modern. Because of this, I find it easiest to explain what magic is to newbies using chaos magic, even if it's not the form of magic they ultimately want to stick with.

Let's face it, even if we've had magical experiences, or seen a ghost, or want to believe, we live in a world that is fundamentally unmagical. In chaos magic this is called **consensus reality,** which refers to the dominant views about the nature of what is "real" that a culture or group of people has. Ideas about gender, sexuality, money, values, and politics almost all fall under the idea of consensus reality. Another example of a consensus reality is citizenship: whether you are a citizen of this place or that place depends on which side of an imaginary line you were born, and that line only really exists because we all believe it does. It takes years of what's called **deconditioning** through ritual and reshaping your thoughts to break from consensus reality and begin to take a bit of your destiny into your own hands, magically speaking. The language and philosophy of chaos magic, in my experience, help you do this and are designed to make magic accessible.

Emerging in the UK in the 1970s alongside the punk movement, chaos magic took a radical approach to the occult that was somewhat controversial at the time. Chaos magicians weren't concerned with fancy robes, ancient orders, or climbing levels of initiation. Instead, they said that anyone can do magic—in fact, we all do it all the time—and that the actual "tech" of doing magic is basically the same all over the world, just in different costumes. Whether you agree with this last part or not, I commend chaos magic for breaking down the door of the temple and letting regular people inside.

Chaos magic isn't religious, and it isn't particularly concerned with morality. It's about breaking magic down into a technology, in the process figuring out what makes magic work and discarding everything that doesn't. It's an eclectic practice, in which gods are given the same level of importance as rock stars, pop culture figures, and fictional characters, and reality is seen as a field of overlapping belief systems. Navigating this landscape of the mind is where chaos magic thrives.

In this chapter, we're going to look at the core principles, ideas, and history of chaos magic. My hope is that these ideas will help make magic real to you and that you keep them in mind as we proceed through the rest of this book. As we go, we'll be covering some weird topics and difficult concepts that trip a lot of people up. My hope is that understanding the principles of chaos magic will make grasping and practicing other forms of magic easier for you.

So why do some people spell magic as *magik*, or even *magick* if you are feeling spicy? This spelling started up in the nineteenth century and gained popularity in the twentieth as a way to distinguish stage magic from spiritual practices. The idea is that stage magicians are tricksters and performers doing tasks that are actually impossible, while magicians in the magickal sense are using ritual to expand consciousness and use unknown natural laws to do what *seems* impossible, but is entirely possible through magick.

I'll be honest: the whole thing is a little silly to me. It reminds me of the "we demand to be taken seriously" joke from *Arrested Development*. If you like it or think the distinction is one that needs to be made, then by all means use *magick* to your heart's content. I personally trust that you understand I have absolutely no idea how to saw someone in half.

CHAOS IN A NUTSHELL

Chaos magic is highly individualized and shirks dogma of all kinds, so it can be hard to pin down what chaos magic is in totality. Some basic principles Phil Hine outlines in his outstanding book *Condensed Chaos* help us get to the heart of chaos:

NO DOGMA

Chaos magicians reject dogma, strict ideas, or any assumption that rules need to be followed. The only exception might be if strict adherence to rules helps you achieve a magical goal.

A RELIANCE ON PERSONAL EXPERIENCE

You must actually *do* magic to get good at it. How you do magic, and which exercises you practice, might not look like what other people are doing, but a certain level of discipline is required to get good at anything—and magic is no exception. Additionally, if something works for you that people say "shouldn't" or is impossible, pay them no mind and do your own thing.

DECONDITION YOURSELF

As I mentioned before, we're born into a world that throws all sorts of ideas at us about who we are and what we should do with our lives. You need to break away from these ideas to see which ones serve you, which ones don't, and ultimately become less attached to ideas and dogma in general.

DIVERSE APPROACHES

Everyone is different, and what works for one person might not work for another. The goal isn't to force someone to do magic your way or to force yourself into what you think you "should" be doing. Instead, your goal is, through trial and error, to figure out what works for you.

GNOSIS

This word is used differently in chaos magic than in other forms of magic we'll cover later. For chaos magicians, *gnosis* is the ability to shift your consciousness at will. We all shift our consciousness when we sleep, drink alcohol, or zone out on long drives, but doing this at will helps you get into a magical state of mind.

IT'S ALL ABOUT RESULTS

Chaos magic came about during a time when the occult scene in the UK was dominated by Wicca, Thelema, and remnants of the Golden Dawn and nineteenth-century occultism. These religions and groups, as we'll learn in later chapters, often had very specific ideas about what magic is and how to do it. Things like ceremonial magic (see chapter 5) have elaborate rituals for just about everything—from making a wand to picking that wand up to using that wand to putting it back down—and, no, I'm not exaggerating. People at the time believed, and many still do, that if you didn't do all these rituals perfectly and weren't initiated into the right magical orders, then magic simply wouldn't work for you.

As a reaction against this, people started taking a DIY approach, grounded in the idea that magic is something anyone can do. Chaos magic is a very personal and customizable practice, as opposed to a cookie-cutter one. Through studying chaos magic, you're in many ways studying yourself. Maybe you get better results from a spell by following the formula to a T, or maybe it works just as well if you substitute in new ingredients, chants, gestures, and so forth. One reason why keeping a magical journal (like we talked about on page 28) is important is so you can track these results and see what works for you.

BELIEF AS A TOOL

One of the central ideas of chaos magic is that belief is a tool, rather than an absolute state, and ideas are only as good as they are useful to you.

When you are driving down a road and come to a red light, you stop. There's nothing about the light itself that makes you stop, instead it's your belief in the red light and what it means that makes you do that. If you look around and run that red light because you think the coast is clear, but then get pulled over, it's the collective belief in the law that makes the ticket you're about to get such a drag. The ticket itself is just a piece of paper with squiggles on it, and the cop is just a guy in a costume.

People often bring up something like the placebo effect to disprove magic, saying "it's all in your head!" Chaos magic reframes this disbelief, taking it as proof that magic is, in fact, real. Let's look at an example with the placebo effect to see how that plays out. Imagine you take a pill that you believe will make you happy, and then you are. When the pill turns out to be just sugar, rather than a "real" mood elevator, that actually proves the presence of magic—because it was your own inner power that made your feelings and behavior change, not the pill.

What chaos magic tries to do is hack this process, maximizing its benefits. If wearing fancy robes and chanting Latin words makes your magic work, then do it! If it doesn't, then try something else. The trick is to recognize that you are adopting a belief, and then to believe it with your whole heart in order to make it work.

Belief doesn't just affect your own personal reality or body. Belief defines what reality is and what is possible inside it. The philosopher Thomas Kuhn, whose ideas greatly influenced chaos magic, pointed out that after the Copernican Revolution, stargazers in Europe suddenly discovered the planet Uranus, as well as many other comets and stars. However, in China, where a geocentric worldview wasn't a prevailing belief and ideas about the stars were different, people had been studying Uranus and these other stars for years. Uranus didn't suddenly appear in Europe; people's belief kept them from seeing it.

As you go through this book, keep this story in mind. You're going to be reading about a lot of weird stuff, and some of it might not make sense to you. Try putting on different belief hats, if you will, and see if shifting your perspective makes your magic better or brings things into clearer focus.

For instance, we'll be talking a lot about the origins of different religions and occult ideas. Explaining the birth of these things can often lead people to reject them. They might say that these religions and their claims are fake. (Spoiler: people in the nineteenth century didn't know as much about ancient Egypt as we do, and there are no ancient Wiccans.) But instead of jumping to conclusions, I want you to observe your beliefs and how they affect your magic as you study.

One specific example that's worth looking at is the origin of Wicca (something we'll explore in more depth in chapter 6). A lot of people, including me, initially put up their noses when they learn its origin story and look down on the whole "fake" religion. Observing Wicca from a different angle—one more rooted in the ideas of chaos magic—can change that reaction, though. In my own life, I've met several Wiccan priestesses who have real power, can do incredible things with magic, and host very moving rituals. They know the history of Wicca and the problems within their own religion, but because they can use the belief of an ancient goddess cult as a tool, they can make things happen. If it works and you aren't harming anyone, go for it.

Here's another, more personal, example: I rejected Aleister Crowley and his ideas for a long time. I knew he was a jerk, and I didn't get along well with people who were *really* into his stuff. I wrote him—and his religion of Thelema—off for years as just another overhyped white guy. However, in an effort to understand the hype, I gave his work a shot. I let myself adopt the belief that he was a prophet and his magic would make my life better. And you know what? My life got better.

I think context is important because it informs and deepens your magical practice. (I also think knowing your history keeps you from being grifted by a cult leader who claims to be an Atlantean goddess.) As you move forward in your studies, remember that belief and your own personal context can be driving forces of magic.

As you read this book, think about how you think and what beliefs serve your life and your magic. What are the mental conditions you need to be in to make your magic work best? What model works best for you?

PARADIGMS

The same philosopher I mentioned earlier, Thomas Kuhn, coined the term *paradigm* to describe a prevailing belief of a culture or person. Chaos magic picked this idea up and ran with it, describing three different major paradigms or models that magic typically falls into.

THE SPIRIT MODEL

This was the prevailing model for most of the history of magic. With the spirit model, spirits are real beings with motives and minds of their own. Spirits aren't metaphors, with vampires representing greed or ghosts representing lingering sadness. Instead, they are things to be guarded against or spoken to through the use of symbols, tools, and ritual.

THE PSYCHOLOGICAL MODEL

This is the model that is usually easiest for modern people to grasp, and it's one that a lot of people beginning their occult studies today choose to adopt. If you are explaining magic to someone, this might be the easiest framework to use. The psychological model maintains that all gods, spirits, and monsters are reflections of our own subconscious and any magical work done with these beings is a way to hack our own brains.

Let's say you have a problem with anger. You fly into a rage at the smallest things, and it's starting to hurt your life and relationships. Under this model, you might imagine you are possessed by a demon of anger and perform an exorcism of this "demon" on yourself.

Thinkers like Joseph Campbell and Carl Jung espoused this model, with myths and legends being metaphors for human psychology, rather than literal events, or coded magical ideas.

THE ENERGY MODEL

I'd like to state for the record that I think we should change the name of this model to "the vibes model." Popular in the nineteenth and early twentieth century, this model sees the universe as the resonance of energy. This model is often referenced in relation to auras, energy work, prana, chi, or, like I said, vibes. The idea is that everyone and everything gives off an energy field and working with those fields is what magic is.

While you read and work with this book, consider which model best works for you, and which ones you might already use to define your reality. It's worth mentioning that you can switch between different models, and that each model has pros and cons.

Most chaos magicians say you should pick a model and stick with it to make your magic most effective, but it's also good to keep yourself limber, magically speaking. To do this in terms of chaos magic, you'll perform what's called a *paradigm shift*.

PARADIGM SHIFT

A paradigm shift is a fancy way of saying a change in worldview. Think about times in your life when you've really had your mind blown, when you learned or experienced something that fundamentally changed how you see reality. You experienced a paradigm shift!

Traditionally, to instigate a paradigm shift, you must go through something known as an *initiation* or a shift in consciousness caused by ritual or a profound experience. But within chaos magic, since perspective is the core of this magic, the ability to shift paradigms at will makes you a good magician.

A small example might be something like this: There are things you might say, do, and act on at home that you wouldn't at work. Maybe there are jokes you tell with your roommate, clothes you wear, or just ways you generally behave that would garner some strange looks from your boss. When you go from home to work, then home again, you are shifting paradigms, even if only a little. Expand this into societal shifts around big philosophical and political ideas over time, and you start to get a sense for what this feels like.

SIGILS

Another popular idea from chaos magic—and an idea that we will expand upon in the activity at the end of this chapter—is that of sigils. Sigils are like programmed thoughtforms that you create through art. They work the same way stop signs, green lights, and notifications work to subconsciously shape our reality. Once you have a thought like "I love my new house" or "I'm happily married" programmed into a sigil, it's amazing how quickly reality forms around that idea.

The typical method for making sigils comes from comic book author Grant Morrison. You begin by writing a present-tense statement of something you want, like "I have a new house that I love living in" or "I am making more than enough money to support myself." You then take out the vowels and repeating letters and put the leftover consonants together to make a symbol. After you make your symbol, you have to charge it with intent by performing a ritual to wake it up, strongly visualizing your goal while you do so.

After you have your sigil, place it somewhere you will passively see it every day, like your mirror or behind your front door. By placing your sigil in such a common place, it will manifest your desire by implanting the idea of the reality you want in your subconscious, the same way a stoplight automatically makes you stop.

Sigils are a great way to get started in magic and spell craft if you aren't very experienced. They're also great to do even if you are! If you want to get your magical sea legs before you try some of the other activities in this book, try making some sigils and see what happens.

CASE STUDY: LADY GAGA

I'm really going to show my nerd hand on this one, but I don't care. It's my book, damn it, and I'll use pop stars as examples of wizards if I like.

I think Lady Gaga is an interesting modern example of what using chaos magic can look like. (Donald Trump is another one, but I'm trying to keep the mood light.) She's also a particularly interesting example of how you don't necessarily need to consciously know you are doing magic in order to do it.

When asked about her success in early interviews, Lady Gaga would often say that just a few years ago she didn't have a ton of money and she wasn't famous, but she would wake up every day and pretend she was famous. She ritualized this idea by writing songs about having money and fame and by acting like she was already famous, until one day she woke up and really was famous.

Lady Gaga, especially the early incarnation of her, is a character that a woman named Stefani Germanotta created. In chaos magic you might call this creating both a **hypersigil** and a **servitor.** A hypersigil is like a sigil, but you create it through performance pieces or storytelling. A servitor is a sigil that is created and fed for a specific, long-term purpose, which takes on a life of its own (more on those later). Lady Gaga getting onstage and saying that she came from nothing but worked hard and became a superstar is her creating a story, or hyper-sigil, for her life and then living that story. In reality, she went to private schools her whole life and had a supportive family on the Upper West Side of New York City. That's not exactly nothing, but remember that reality is what you make of it.

In this case, Stefani Germanotta created the servitor of Lady Gaga and told it (maybe not explicitly), "Make me rich and famous," then fed it through ritual (i.e., concerts, performances, and parties). Eventually, when she became famous, the character of Lady Gaga didn't belong to her anymore. It went from being a servitor, to an **egregore,** or a thoughtform shared and created by many people. Things that aren't "real" but are made real and take on a life of their own through the course of many people believing in them are egregores. Things like the United States of America, Hollywood, or Disney are all egregores.

What happens when a spell no longer belongs to you? What happens when an egregore as a living idea is bound to you and your life forever? I think a lot of celebrities, not just Lady Gaga, go through this, and I think it's one reason why so many of them end up with mental health issues. In recent interviews, Gaga has spoken about how her life had been taken over by this character she could no longer control. She's spoken openly about how she contemplated suicide and spent nights yelling at her old piano, angry that it was the magical tool that conjured Lady Gaga into existence. When magic gets out of hand, it can be very painful and destructive.

I don't bring this up to scare you away from magic or to make you think that it always leads to bad things. Rather, I think it's important to keep this story in mind when you practice chaos magic as both a demonstration of magic's power and as a cautionary tale. Reality is malleable, changing your thoughts and solidifying them with ritual can change your life, and everything is permitted. However, in accepting that magic is real, you accept that you must take respon-sibility for its role in your life.

HISTORY

While most of this book is based strongly in history, this chapter is more focused on exploring the ideas of chaos magic and their influence. That's because chaos magicians themselves don't often place much emphasis on their history, seeing context as unimportant and results as the only things that matter in magic.

However, in the interest of consistency, and perhaps a bit of clarity, I'm going to outline a brief history of chaos magic and its major figures.

While chaos magic was officially created in the 1970s, its roots stretch back much further.

Austin Osman Spare was a late nineteenth-century artist and occultist who is considered by most to be the grandfather of chaos magic. While ideas about sigil magic can arguably be traced back to ancient runes and Scandinavian magic, Spare coined the term *sigil* and created the modern idea of using symbols and art to program thoughtforms. While a brilliant thinker, his books are a difficult read, and I personally don't think you have to go back and flip through them to grasp what he was talking about.

Another figure who can be credited as a proto-chaos magician—and someone whom we will talk about more in later chapters—is Aleister Crowley. Crowley believed magic wasn't something only a select few people could, or should, learn. Instead, he saw it as part of the fabric of reality. He famously begins his book *Magick in Theory and Practice* with the line "Magick is for ALL" and encouraged his students to experiment with ritual to figure out what worked best for them as individuals.

Flash forward about a half century. Two world wars have been fought, several major revolutions have been attempted (with mixed success), and, in the UK specifically, the largest empire in world history up until that point was humiliated and economically depressed. With all this in the background, it became, and has remained, hard for people to believe like they used to. The old paradigms just didn't work anymore, but in the magical world, people kept going on like the old rituals and orders could be maintained exactly as they had with little change.

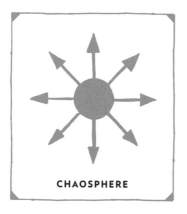

CHAOSPHERE

Just as punk musicians decided to give a middle finger to the old way of doing things, many magicians and occultists decided magic was long overdue for a revolution. Peter Carroll is widely credited with creating the modern chaos magic movement with his book *Liber Null*, even though the book doesn't use the phrase "chaos magic" anywhere in the text. Later, magicians and writers like Phil Hine, William S. Burroughs, Genesis P-Orridge, and Robert Anton Wilson would further expand and play with the ideas of chaos magic through their own writings, music, and art.

Early chaos magicians were inspired by sci-fi and horror writers like H. P. Lovecraft and Michael Moorcock and the TV show *Star Trek*. Moorcock's Eternal Champion series gives chaos magic what might be the closest thing it has to an official symbol: the Chaosphere.

Early on, chaos magic incubated a very small, very silly movement called *discordianism*. You don't find too many discordians these days, but I still find them funny enough to mention. Discordianism is a religion (or a parody of religion) started in California in the 1960s with the publication of the book *Principia Discordia*. Discordians worship Eris, the Greek goddess of chaos, and hold, among other beliefs, that everyone is pope and hot dogs should be consumed every Friday, but also that it's a sin to eat hot dogs. It's a religion that leans in hard to the absurdity of life and tries to find joy in chaos.

Chaos magic has made a lot of inroads into pop culture over the years, from Grant Morrison's *The Invisibles* to shout-outs in the Marvel Cinematic Universe (MCU) from Doctor Strange and the Scarlet Witch.

JOURNAL PROMPTS

◆ What are some core beliefs I have? Where did I get these beliefs from? Do they serve me?

◆ What is the paradigm of the culture I live in? What parts of this belief system do I like or dislike?

◆ Write down times in your life when your perspective changed. Is there something in common about them? What caused you to change your mind?

◆ Throughout your day, try to pick out moments when you are interacting with beliefs as reality. For instance, gravity seems pretty real whether a bunch of people believe in it or not, but does money?

◆ Write down characters, mythological figures, or celebrities who inspire you. What are the traits about them you would like to embody?

MAKING A SERVITOR

So what is a servitor? Well, it's basically an inspirited sigil or thoughtform—one that you give a name and maybe even a personality. You'll have a more hands-on relationship with a servitor than you would with a normal sigil. While sigils might be good for specific, unusual problems, servitors are good for long-term help. You're essentially making a little spirit, familiar, or mental computer program—depending on your magical model—that can handle tasks and work for you on specific requests. You'll feed this servitor by creating a sigil and making a small altar or space for it to "live," where you can leave offerings when it comes through for you.

For example, let's say you drive for a living and have a hard time finding parking in the city or town where you reside. You could create a sigil out of the phrase "I am always able to find parking," if you like you can give it a name (literally something as simple as "Heck yes" so you can easily and covertly thank it when you find parking), and set up a little altar in your car or garage. You can already see how this is a little less intimidating than summoning an ancient demon to find you parking.

For this activity, you will need:

Paper

A pen or marker

A glass of water

Other art supplies like glitter, glue, images from magazines or the internet, etc. (optional)

Making a servitor has several steps. The first is crafting a sigil, so let's go over that process quickly.

Figure out a statement of intent, or something you want the servitor to do. Keep it simple, present tense, and positive, like "gigs come easily to me" or "lots of great people want to date me." Remember, you can always make others down the line to add specificity.

✦ *Take out all the vowels and repeating letters.*

✦ *Arrange the remaining letters into a symbol.*

✦ *Make the symbol look cool by drawing it in the colors and style you think suit it.*

Now, keep in mind that while a normal sigil is great for one-off problems, like finding a new apartment, servitors are better for tasks you'll need help with on a regular basis. Once you have your sigil, feel free to make it as artistic and crazy as you want. There really are no rules here, and in fact I think it's best to let your imagination go wild, whether that's making a collage, a painting, macaroni art, or whatever else your heart desires.

After you have your sigil, the next step is charging it. I like the word *charging* because it has two magical meanings. In one sense, you are imbuing an object with energy or power, like charging a battery. In another sense, you are giving this object a charge, or duty, to perform.

There are lots of ways to charge a sigil—or any object for that matter. Dancing around it, singing to it, burning incense, or any number of creative things all work to charge

sigils, if they work for you. For now, I'm going to share a simple technique that I've found works well for most beginners.

✦ *Sit comfortably and allow yourself to take several deep, calming breaths.*

✦ *Hold the sigil in your hands.*

✦ *Close your eyes and imagine a warm light coming up from the very core of the earth. It slowly travels up your spinal cord until it rests in the center of your chest.*

✦ *Now, imagine another light that descends from above and travels down your spine to meet the first beam of light.*

✦ *Your body fills with light, and you slowly start to push that light out of your body into the sigil.*

✦ *Once you feel your sigil is properly charged, open your eyes and hold it up to you.*

✦ *Give it instructions for what its purpose will be, perhaps even just restating your goal or desire.*

The final, and longest, step will be setting up an altar for this servitor to live on and deciding what kind of offerings to leave it. This doesn't have to be complicated—I recommend

just a glass of water and maybe a candle or two when you are first getting started. Let this servitor know what the deal is: that you'll leave it a glass of water once a week and better offerings when it delivers on its mission statement.

If the time comes when you no longer need this servitor, then it's more than okay to let it go. In fact, it would be kind of rude to just forget about it. Thank it for the work it has done for you and leave it a final offering. Then, you can bury it at a crossroads, burn it, or dispose of it in a way you think is fitting for the task.

FURTHER READING

The Complete Psychonaut Field Manual: A Cartoon Guide to Chaos Magick
This free webcomic on the Ultraculture website is a great introduction to chaos magic, especially if you are visually minded. Basic concepts, rituals, and operations are laid out in a clear and entertaining way.

Condensed Chaos, Phil Hine
This is a book I recommend to pretty much every newbie who comes to me asking where they should get started with magic. A foundational text on chaos magic, Hine's work does a really good job defining magic in accessible language. Read this book.

Six Ways, Aidan Wachter
I could technically recommend this book at the end of several chapters, since Wachter's approach to magic fits nicely into witchcraft, folk magic, and grimoire traditions. However, since he's officially a chaos magician, the recommendation goes here. A deceptively short book, this volume is packed with straightforward magical wisdom and knowledge. Absolutely anyone—whether new to magic or a seasoned practitioner—can benefit from this book.

SPELL BOOKS
AND
GRIMOIRES

Spell books are some of the most iconic images to be conjured up when someone mentions magic. From *Buffy the Vampire Slayer* to *Hocus Pocus* and *Evil Dead,* spell books remain such a widespread trope in pop culture that people are sometimes surprised to find out they are real!

For centuries, magical knowledge was passed down in handwritten books called grimoires, which taught people how to summon spirits, cast spells, divine the future, and even find buried treasure.

So what is a grimoire? It's a little hard to define, and there are disagreements between experts (shocker), but broadly speaking: The name *grimoire* comes from the French word *gramarie,* which means "almanac" or "handbook." Grimoires are essentially handbooks of magic. "But," you might be thinking, "what makes a book like the one I have in my hands a book about magic, and not a grimoire?" That, my friend, is where things get fun. Grimoires often contain a list of spirits, ways to call them, and reasons why you might want to call them. Each grimoire has slightly different ways of doing this, and some are basically one long book about how to do a single magical operation. The different methods for calling spirits are largely what separates one spell book from another.

Many grimoires are situated within a system of magic known as **Goetia**. This is another word that's a little tough to define—some say it comes from the ancient Greek word for sorcery, while others link it to the Greek words *goes,* "a howler of enchantments," and *goëtes,* "a group of professional wailers for a funeral in ancient Greece" (things used to be cooler).

Either way, Goetia is certainly very tied to the history of witchcraft in Europe during the Middle Ages. If you were caught in possession of grimoires, that was often enough to sentence you to death for the crime of witchcraft, as was the case with Hew Draper, a sixteenth-century shopkeeper who was imprisoned in the Tower of London after being accused of owning a collection of spell books and whose astrological graffiti can still be seen in the cell where he was imprisoned.

The symbols and tools of the grimoires can also occasionally be seen in art. My favorite example of this is a sixteenth-century painting called *The Witches' Cove*, in which a coven of cats can be seen dancing near magical seals.

Broadly speaking, a book of Goetia is something that relates to demons and demon summoning. There is a wide range of reasons why someone would do this today (which we'll get into more in a bit), but ancient magicians summoned

demons for two primary reasons: some sought to bring forth demons for practical reasons like wealth and power, while others did so as a test of faith, like looking at a lot of expensive things online and then deleting the tabs before you buy anything.

There is no central or definitive grimoire, and grimoires often contradict each other. However, some people and characters pop up consistently in grimoires across history. Names like King Solomon or St. Cyprian can be found across cultures and time, which points to the ways in which grimoires acted as a living tradition, or at least something that resembles a very long and drawn out version of a game of telephone.

If this book had existed about twenty years ago, it's likely that this chapter wouldn't have made it in. Despite being a core component of European, North African, and Middle Eastern magic for almost two thousand years, grimoires fell out of popularity in the twentieth century, which is why you won't see them mentioned much in introductory magic books, even though they are more available now than at any point in history. In recent years, however, people have begun a movement that's being called "the grimoire revival," in which these old spell books are being dusted off and seen in a new light.

I want to pause for a moment to look at how grimoires fit into a pattern that will keep coming up during this course of study. Throughout this book, we'll spend a lot of time unpacking the supposed origin myths of religions, groups, and ideas to try to go back to where they actually come from for clarity. The hot take I have come to while writing this book, the thing I will be repeating many more times, and the thesis on the occult I've come to during all this study, is that the only thing that unites all corners of occultism is the desire to ground oneself in an earlier, mythic age. Whether it's Atlantis, Avalon, or ancient Egypt, lots of people claim that their ideas come directly from some ancient source when, in reality, they are either kidding themselves or you. I want to note that this isn't in and of itself a bad thing, and in the case of some grimoires it might have been done to hide authorship from hostile authorities.

The thing about the grimoires, though, is that while they often do claim mythic origins, there is also a very clear historical link that we can follow back through time, sometimes as far back as ancient Greece, Egypt, and Sumer! The chain isn't unbroken, but the links are there, and if you are interested in your practice being informed by history or placing it inside a living tradition, I recommend you try to incorporate things from the grimoires into the magic you do.

I get very excited when I think of a group of young, smart, diverse people picking up the spell books of old because for a long time they've just sort of sat there. Part of that has to do with access, because these books have historically been hard to find and only the nerds of yore have been keeping the tradition alive. However, even in an age of PDFs and instant everything, it's been difficult for people interested in magic to get into these texts.

There are a few barriers to entry for people new to studying the grimoires. It can be difficult to know exactly what you're looking at when you pick one up, and the astrological, alchemical, herbal, and mythological knowledge that goes into deciphering them can make it feel like you'll never know enough to even begin. While I think it's important to have some basic magical knowledge under your belt before diving into grimoire magic, I'm personally against the idea of what my friend Charles Porterfield calls "strange anti-magical prohibitions"— by which he means the illogical idea that you can only start to "really" do magic when you have everything exactly right and are already a superpowerful magician. Or, that if you do even one thing wrong when you are starting out, then certain doom awaits you. Everyone needs to start somewhere, and while I'm not saying you should throw all caution to the wind and begin summoning demons willy-nilly, I also don't want you to keep yourself from doing magic because of a vague sense that you "aren't ready." Spoiler: that feeling never really goes away, so just go for it.

Another barrier to doing grimoire magic, especially for new students, is that there are very few books written for and by actual magical practitioners on the subject. This is changing slowly, but for a long time all you had was a PDF of the actual grimoire or scholarly books written by people who don't actually practice magic. This meant that you would either have no context for what you were looking at or only context without any practical knowledge.

I'm going to attempt to break down these barriers in this chapter. Since this isn't a book on grimoires, a lot is going to be left out, but what I hope to do is make the landing a little less bumpy when you do open a JSTOR article or buy an original text. My hope is that if you know what you're looking at when you pick up one of these books, you'll feel freer to try spells out and get creative.

HISTORY

It would take me well over the word count my publisher gave me to go into the history of every grimoire ever written. So instead, I'm going to go over *some* of the history, highlight a few greatest hits, and give you the tools to know what you are looking at next time you are in a particularly good occult bookstore.

While magic has existed forever, spell books have not. Depending on cultural ideas about writing, language, and books, people have either treated writing down magical knowledge as a spell in and of itself or a thing that makes magic lose all potency. The antecedents of the grimoires emerged out of Ptolemaic Egypt, where writing was sometimes seen as sacred and books and scrolls were not just record-keeping instruments but ritual tools as well.

We don't really know what the first grimoire was, but we have some good ideas about what older spell books looked like. The Greek Magical Papyri (or PGM) are a good example of a collection of magic scrolls and writings that comes from late antiquity and has survived in bits and pieces up to the present day.

In medieval Jewish, Christian, and Islamic lore, Adam, the first man, is sometimes given credit as the first magician and the first author of magical books. However, far more popular is the figure Enoch (known as Idris in Arabic) who was said to have recorded the first angelic and astrological lore in history. This knowledge, the legend goes, was passed down to Noah and later Moses, all of whom were seen as powerful magicians. You can see where the history we are talking about is at the same time material and mythic.

Historically speaking, in the BCE period paper had not yet been introduced into what is now Europe from Asia, and the printing press wasn't invented until 1450. This meant books had to be handwritten on papyrus, parchment, or other expensive materials, which in turn made books and written works prized and highly priced items—spell books even more so. But who was writing spell books during the Middle Ages, a time when practicing magic could land you in jail or worse?

Well, ironically enough, a lot of monks! There was something called "The Clerical Underground," which sounds like a band but actually refers to the many monks and priests who copied grimoires in secret. There was a bit of a debate at the time as to which sorts of magic were an affront to God and which weren't, with many seeing "natural" magic, or magic used to uncover the hidden secrets of nature, as a good thing. Remember, Isaac Newton was an alchemist *and* a scientist—these things weren't so different back in the day.

This is also something important to keep in mind when you study grimoire magic, or the ceremonial magic that grows out of it. The people writing and copying these books were working on monk time, meaning they didn't have to make money, work long hours, take care of families, or waste hours shopping online. As a result, some of the spells and rituals you find in these books can take days to do, because why not? What else have you got going on? You're a monk! Now, I don't want to say you can always disregard instructions in grimoires and make up your own timeline for everything, but you will likely have to adjust some things to make room for non-monk time.

In the early modern period, paper and the invention of the printing press allowed for books to be printed, distributed, and made more accessible than ever before. Historians often point to the Protestant Reformation as a direct result of the printing press, and while that's important in a grand historical sense, what's critical for us in this book is that the printing press led to what's often called "the democratization of magic."

In a pre-press world, books were difficult to make and cost a lot of money. After the invention of the printing press, they could suddenly be made and distributed with ease. Pamphlets, almanacs, and books of magic flooded Europe, with the previously handwritten books and secrets of old copied into print. At last, you didn't have to be a rich person living in a castle or monastery somewhere to own spell books. Common people incorporated magic from the grimoires into preexisting folk practices, including using planetary timing and magical seals.

Now, a lot of grimoires were mistranslated, copied wrong, or reprinted with symbols upside down or backward. This process actually helps us date when certain grimoires were written or appeared in certain countries, the same way that you can date posts online to pre/post 2005 if they use the phrase "do not want." These differences in grimoires have led to some debate among people who practice grimoiric magic around which translations are accurate and which books are more or less legit than others. At this point in your studies, I wouldn't worry about all that, but know that debates like this persist until the present.

At the same time magical books were flooding Europe, the Protestant Reformation and the Enlightenment—both made possible by the printing press—were helping fuel a backlash against magic. Witch trials swept across Europe for the rest of the early modern period, with possession of spell books sometimes used as evidence that a person was practicing witchcraft.

For about a century, the writing and study of grimoires went largely quiet. It wasn't until the occult revival of the nineteenth century that these books, as well as magic in general, were picked up as a popular practice. The translation of the Rosetta Stone, in particular, helped reawaken interest in old spell books and ancient writings. In the United States, Joseph Smith supposedly used grimoire magic to channel the Book of Mormon. Later in the century, over in England, occultists Aleister Crowley and Samuel Mathers completed new translations of the Key of Solomon and the Greek Magical Papyri.

The twentieth century saw a move away from grimoires and spell books in favor of postmodern forms of magic like chaos magic. The early twenty-first century, however, has seen the grimoire revival, in which people are dusting off these old books and seeing what wisdom can be gleaned from them. This sometimes takes the form of postcolonial work, a reinvigorated interest in animism, and an inspirited worldview.

And all that brings us here. Part of the reason I wanted to include this chapter in an introductory occultism book is because I think these volumes have collected dust for quite long enough. I believe grimoires are meant to be read and used, particularly by people who need their help. Grimoire work has been looked at as an advanced form of magic for a while now, and while I agree there's some advanced stuff in these books, I think some of this attitude comes from the fact that there are very few easy introductions to this magic. My hope for this chapter, and this book in general, is that it starts a second democratization of magic and makes you feel less intimidated about giving grimoires a try.

Now that we've taken a broad look at the history of magical books, let's dive in and explore some of the A-list titles.

CHOOSING A GRIMOIRE

The best way to get into grimoire magic is to pick a book that sounds appealing to you and try out a bunch of the spells and rituals it contains. If you don't like the vibe of it, you can always switch to a different one, and if you really like it, stick with it—don't feel pressured to master every book of magic ever written.

Take a moment to think back to what I asked at the start of this book: what do you want to get out of magic? Do you want to talk to spirits and gods? Do you want practical spells that will materially improve your life? Do you want to deepen your spirituality for its own sake? It's okay if you want a little of each! All the following books will contain a little of each of these things, but some will have greater emphasis on one or another. Thinking about what you are looking for, magically speaking, will greatly help in narrowing down your search for a grimoire.

Before going through these books, I want to address a few things that throw a lot of people off when they are studying grimoires. The first is the idea of demons. They don't pop up in every grimoire, but they certainly make an appearance in a lot of them. I've seen a lot of people become interested in grimoires, read the word *demon,* and run away screaming with visions from horror movies playing in their heads.

I don't want to downplay the idea that demons can seriously fuck your shit up, but I want to take a minute to put the term in context and offer a slightly different way of viewing them. For a while, *demon, devil,* and *spirit* were used more or less interchangeably. The word *demon* itself comes from the Greek *daimon,* which basically means "spirit," but which was used to describe everything from gods to ghosts. Remember, grimoires were written in all sorts of languages and went through many translations. Some of them date back thousands of years, before the idea of Christian demons was even around. A demon like Baal, for instance, was originally the Canaanite god of fertility. Other demons, like Stolas, a cute owl that teaches people about rocks and poisonous plants, don't seem "demonic" at all.

I once heard someone say that if you aren't scared, you aren't really doing magic, and I do agree with this to a certain degree. It's good to push our boundaries and make ourselves uncomfortable from time to time, and at the end of the day, magic is considered spooky because it can be really spooky! I don't want you to see a scary word like *demon* and immediately stop pursuing magic. However, I also understand that this is simply too big a hurdle for some people to cross—and if you are one of those people, that's okay! Goetia (demon stuff) isn't something I recommend beginners jump into—in fact I generally caution against it—but I don't want you to feel intimidated before you even begin.

This is where the divination and meditative techniques we went over in chapter 2 come in. If you are unsure if you should work with a particular demon or spirit, or if you have been working with one and you feel like it's negatively impacting your life in some way, check in through divination or meditation. You aren't a fake magician if you decide not to work with these entities, and you aren't suddenly going to become the main character of a horror movie if you do.

The second issue people often run into when working with spell books is the long list of strange and seemingly impossible items that grimoires sometimes ask you to use. The first time I picked up a grimoire I read that I needed to sacrifice a black rooster at midnight and promptly put the book back down. Exactly how was I, a fifteen-year-old girl at the time, supposed to get my hands on and sacrifice a black rooster?

Here's the deal: you can cut some corners with these books. I don't think you should cut *every* corner, but there are some objects and tasks that are simply impossible for most modern people to acquire and perform. In cases like this, I recommend you do your best to get the supplies that are within your grasp and get creative with the ones that aren't. Think poetically and symbolically. If a spell asks for a belt made of lion's skin, and for some reason you can't get that, could you use a faux leopard-skin belt instead? If a book asks for a rooster to sacrifice, can you instead smash or destroy an image of a rooster? Once again, I don't want the strangeness of these spell books to make you feel like you can't do magic or cause you to worry that something will go horrifically wrong if you don't do things 100 percent "right." In fact, in my experience spirits tend to appreciate that you are making an effort at all and will admire your creativity.

The last thing that throws some people off is that many of these books begin with some sort of warning. They'll say that you should turn back from reading or something horrible will happen to you! People often read these and, understandably, get scared and put the book down.

Have you ever walked into a place that said, "No Trespassing" or "Beware of Dog"? These warnings are a bit like that. These books often contained secrets that magicians didn't want others getting hold of, and they were also often illegal to possess. At the time many of these books were written, you risked being tortured or killed if you were found with a bunch of spell books in your possession.

With this context in mind, the presence of some warnings is understandable. However, just as there sometimes isn't any dog to be afraid of or people around to watch you trespass, some of these warnings can be taken with a grain, or circle, of salt.

I think it's important to always be respectful of spirits and magical books, but respect and fear aren't the same thing. If a book or a spell doesn't speak to you, don't feel pressured to use it. At the same time, make sure you aren't just putting that book down out of fear alone. If you approach grimoires with a respectful attitude and have some basic protection measures memorized, you'll almost certainly be fine.

Now, with that out of the way, let's dive into some popular grimoires.

Grimoires have historically been pretty rare and have only recently begun to be translated and made available to a wider audience. Some are still fairly hard to acquire, and many haven't been transcribed or printed by major publications. To make things accessible for your studies, the following grimoires are all available either for purchase or as free PDFs online. I encourage you to support scholarship on this subject by buying these books, if possible, but I also understand that can't always be done.

THE GREEK MAGICAL PAPYRI

This is one of the oldest collections of spells we have—and it's quite astonishing we have it at all. Called the Greek Magical Papyri (or PGM, Papyri Graecae Magicae in Latin, for short) because of its origin in Ptolemaic Egypt, this book is actually a collection of many magical papyri written between about 100 BCE and 400 CE. Because the PGM is a composite spell book, these scrolls and bits of writing were composed in many different ancient languages and mostly unknown until the early nineteenth century. They were eventually translated into Greek, Latin, and English, at which point historians and occultists alike found great fun in reading through the ancient spells and rituals. Perhaps the most famous one, the Headless Rite—or the Bornless Rite, depending on whom you ask—was incorporated into Aleister Crowley's magical work and appears in the opening pages of his translation of the *Lesser Key of Solomon.*

The PGM doesn't have a central formula for summoning spirits or lots of symbols and magic circles like other grimoires do, but that makes it more accessible in some ways. It serves as a portrait of what magic looked like in the ancient Mediterranean region, with deities like Hekate, Selene, and Hermes dancing through its pages with spells for things like love, victory, and vengeance— it turns out, people haven't changed much in the last couple thousand years. I'm biased because I really like this book, but I think it is a great choice for a first grimoire since it's pretty straightforward.

Because this book isn't a grimoire proper—it's more of an ancestor to the "real" grimoires—it doesn't contain the long formulas or complex rituals that other spell books do. I find this makes it easy to scale up or down in terms of the level of complexity you want. However, since it's a collection of scattered pieces of text, this sometimes makes the PGM physically more difficult to read, even if it's easier to use.

THE PICATRIX

We aren't sure of the exact author or date of this particular grimoire, but it likely comes from around the eleventh century. Translated from Arabic, the title means "The Goal of the Wise."

Originally written in Arabic, this *very* extensive book is one of the earliest spell books we have, and it synthesizes a lot of earlier astrological magic that was happening in the Middle East and Mediterranean Basin.

This book is heavily based around astrology and includes methods of learning astrology, planetary seals, charms, and incantations, as well as herbal, animal, and mineral correspondences to the different planets. It's a long book, and at times a dense read, but if astrology is your thing and you want to learn ways to apply it practically and magically, this is definitely a book you should check out.

LE PETIT ALBERT

One of the most popular grimoires, this small but packed volume was published in the early eighteenth century in France as part of the *bibliothèque bleue,* or blue grimoire, period. A bibliothèque bleue was essentially an old version of a pamphlet, zine, or pulp novel—a cheaply printed and widely distributed book of a dangerous or salacious nature.

I find this book delightful because it contains not only spells and charms, but also recipes for hand soap and face washes, as well as practical farming advice. You really feel transported back to a different time when you are using this grimoire, and it offers insight into how people in the past had very different, while at the same time not so different, needs from our own today.

If you are interested in practical herbal knowledge, homesteading, farming, or just general DIY projects on top of magic, this book is worth reading. If you are also interested in astrological magic and making astrological talismans, this book has a great section on that as well.

THE LESSER KEY OF SOLOMON

This is often the first grimoire that people learn about or encounter. Aleister Crowley translated the text along with Samuel Mathers during his time with the Golden Dawn (see chapter 5), and its importance in the organization made it not only one of the most popular grimoires of the nineteenth century, but of all time. You see it referenced a lot in horror movies—*Hereditary*, *The Conjuring* series, for example—in part because of this popularity.

"Keys of Solomon" are a bit of a subgenre in the grimoire world, meaning you'll find many different books that all have the same or a similar name. Typically, these books have a heavy emphasis on the specific tools you should use and more elaborate rituals than some other grimoires. They also all claim to come from Solomon's magic, in one way or another. If you are just starting out, I recommend the Crowley translation for now.

Like many grimoires, the *Lesser Key of Solomon* contains a long list of spirits, but in my opinion the Crowley translation has one of the more coherent and easy to read lists you'll find. For all of my fellow millennials, I would describe the *Lesser Key of Solomon* as being kind of like a Pokédex of spirits. Inside, you'll find lists of demons, spirits, and beings of the zodiac. Each has their own seal, with which you can summon them, and a brief description of their appearance. It's a strange book that sparks the imagination, with some spirits appearing as the sound of water rushing all around you, men with wings, or a crow.

As we touched on in the chaos magic chapter, Crowley was a bit of a proto-chaos magician, meaning he saw the spirits of the grimoires as psychological ideas and working with them as an extension of your own self. In his introduction to the *Lesser Key*, he says asking a demon to "destroy an enemy" can instead be interpreted as getting rid of the idea of "enemy" and embracing compassion. Likewise, things like "discovering treasure" can mean achieving financial success.

I leave it to you whether you want to work with spirits in this manner or not. Either way, I think it's an interesting idea to sit with, and at the very least can ease a lot of modern people into this kind of magic, which might otherwise be intimidating.

This book is nice for beginners because it has clearly laid out methods of cleansing, banishing, and summoning, but keep in mind that while its way of conjuring spirits is not complicated, it is elaborate. There isn't herbal, plant, or much planetary magic in this book—if you are looking for that specifically, I would search elsewhere. If what you want the most out of magic is the ability to conjure and speak to all sorts of spirits, then this book is worth checking out.

THE SIXTH AND SEVENTH BOOKS OF MOSES

This is the youngest grimoire we'll look at, but it is also one of the most fascinating in terms of its history.

The book claims Moses as its author, though it first appeared in Germany in the nineteenth century. Its true author is hard to determine, and although it purports to be an authentic book about the Talmud and Jewish magic, most scholars side-eye that assertion.

However, all that is not really what makes the *Sixth and Seventh Books of Moses* interesting. In the nineteenth and twentieth centuries this book was printed and distributed widely in the United States, the Caribbean, and West Africa. While some magical practitioners, like the hex doctors and powwow doctors of Pennsylvania, largely saw the book as malignant and even cursed, it was embraced passionately by Black communities and practitioners of hoodoo and rootwork. It remains a popular and important book in these traditions to this day.

This grimoire is less about demons or ancient gods and more about invoking the god of Abraham for healing, guidance, and protection. For a spell book, it feels very religious. If religion is a complex issue for you, I would recommend either trying out another grimoire first or trying to shift your magical model while you use this book. Alternatively, you can look into traditions like hoodoo, rootwork, and folk magic and see how this book is used there.

This book is a perfect example of a concept I introduced at the start of this chapter. Grimoires are living things that are picked up and adapted by different groups of people to meet the needs of the land and themselves. You should feel empowered to do the same. If you are interested in folk magic, specifically American and Black folk magic, then you should read the *Sixth and Seventh Books of Moses*.

FIGURES AND SYMBOLS OF THE GRIMOIRES

While every spell book is different and grimoires aren't a fixed thing with a unified language, there are some symbols and figures found in most grimoires that are worth going over. Below is a list of common symbols, ideas, and figures you're likely to encounter as you study.

KING SOLOMON

When someone is famous, people often lie about knowing them. Your friend being friends with them means you are best friends. Your hanging out a few times means you "go way back."

Because King Solomon of the Bible was seen as the greatest magician of all time (perhaps second to Jesus, depending on whom you ask), many grimoires are attributed to him. Whether this was because people thought they would fool others into believing Solomon penned these books himself, it was done to honor him, or because we are to look at figures like Solomon as currents or spirits who can inspire the work of humans, I leave for you to decide. No matter how you view it, there are enough books credited to him that there is a whole subsection of grimoires that fall under the name "Solomonic magic."

It's hard to overstate how important a figure Solomon was and how big an impact his magic, or magic done in his name, has had on the world. The seal of Solomon, the symbol for Judaism and a

SEAL OF SOLOMON

symbol that you will see often in grimoires, comes from the ring he wore to control demons. As a result, Solomonic magic usually has as a main feature the binding and commanding of demons and spirits.

ST. CYPRIAN

So, back in the day, the Catholic Church was a lot spookier than it is now. Before Vatican II in 1962, when the church reorganized and modernized (sort of) itself, there was more explicit magic and general weirdness in the religion. One of the obvious changes the Catholic Church made to get rid of these magical associations was to alter the charge of several saints. Once upon a time we had St. Clare, the patron saint of psychics. Now? She's the patron saint of television. Also, once upon a time there was a patron saint of magicians and occultists, and his name is St. Cyprian.

Cyprian is credited in many grimoires, mostly from Spain, Portugal, and Southern Europe. He is worth forging a relationship with if you want to work with these books or in heavily Catholic-based magic.

HEINRICH CORNELIUS AGRIPPA

Whether you know it or not, you have encountered this man's work before. From a TikTok video with 200 views explaining color correspondences to the highest-regarded scholarly works, people continue to cite this man's work so often that most don't even know they are doing it.

Heinrich Cornelius Agrippa was a German scholar, physician, and occultist who lived from 1486 to 1535. During his life he published one of the most important book series in all of magical history: *Three Books of Occult Philosophy*. These books, while not grimoires in themselves, synthesized the writings and wisdom of books that came before.

Have you ever wondered why the color orange corresponds to the planet Mercury or why mugwort is considered a "lunar" plant? Agrippa is the reason why. While these ideas existed before him, he collected and standardized them in a way that hadn't really been done before. His work can be a tough read because of the age and complexity of the subject, and I wouldn't suggest it as a 101 book, but if you wish to deepen your occult knowledge or even just historical scholarship, I recommend eventually reading him.

MAGIC CIRCLES

Magic circles are symbols drawn on the floor while you work in order to keep you safe. They usually contain names of God or angels for protection, and sometimes they have another circle within a triangle outside of them for spirits to manifest within.

Something that trips people up about magical circles is that making them as a modern person is somewhat difficult. Lots of spell books talk about drawing

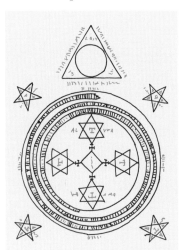

nine-foot-wide circles on the ground, and my New York City apartment is hardly bigger than that.

So what can you do? Well, as with everything in the grimoires, do your best. If you can find a quiet space where you can draw a circle in chalk on the ground, then that's great! If not, try using large sheets of paper, or adjusting the circle to fit the space you have. I would definitely recommend tweaking the dimensions of a magical circle of protection, rather than forgoing it entirely.

MAGIC SEALS

No, not like the sea mammal. Different elements, spirits, and even times of day have their own symbols that you can use to summon them. Think of them like phone numbers or online avatars.

While certain symbols, like planetary glyphs or alchemical symbols, are pretty consistent across magical works, magic seals sometimes change depending on the grimoire you are using. Don't get too hung up on the differences and memorizing every single symbol you encounter. At least in the beginning, just use the seals the grimoire you are working with tells you to, and don't get too fancy by swapping them out with different ones.

NUMBER SQUARES

Also known as *kamea,* magic squares are grids of numbers in which every column and row adds up to the same number. Since planets are associated with different numbers, magic squares are often used to invoke the powers of the seven classical planets (Sun, Moon, Mercury, Venus, Mars, Saturn, Jupiter).

While there are certain ways grimoires will ask that you construct magic squares, a good rule is to make them at the corresponding planetary day and time. You can get creative with this, and make them on paper or use chalk, chalk pens, or permanent markers that correspond with the color of the planet you are invoking. Draw them on an erasable space as you need or put them on a plate or block of wood for a portable altar.

HEBREW LETTERS

We will discuss this more in the next chapter, but beginners sometimes ask why there are so many Hebrew letters used in magic, especially in books written by Christians or Muslims. In the magical system called Kabbalah, every Hebrew letter has a sound, meaning, number, and name associated with it. Like runes, Hebrew letters are seen almost as a mystical DNA or computer code. To keep going with that metaphor, these letters are used to program the signs and symbols used in the grimoires or to bring in the power those letters represent. While this has its roots in Jewish mysticism, a lot of grimoires are fairly far removed from this system, and the Hermetic version of Qabalah is a different thing altogether from Jewish Kabbalah.

Although they are perhaps a more advanced topic, I think it's important for beginners of magic to at least know about the grimoires and what they contain, because they feed into so many other forms of magic. From drawing a magical circle of protection to pentagrams and spooky symbols on T-shirts, you've encountered their wisdom before and just didn't know it! Whether you choose to use them in your practice or not, I hope I've left you with a newfound appreciation for this ancient current of magical knowledge and maybe piqued your interest to try out some new old things.

JOURNAL PROMPTS

- What do I want to gain from magic?
- What are practical areas of my life that I think magic could improve?
- Am I scared to use magic to improve my life? If so, where does that idea come from?
- How do I feel about summoning spirits? Does the idea excite me? Scare me? Why do I think that is?
- What is one book listed above that excites or intrigues me? What small pieces can I break it down into to work with?
- Have I ever interacted with a spirit before, perhaps without realizing it? Something like a strong sense of place or a ghost? How did it make me feel?

MAKING A PLANETARY CANDLE

We've already talked a bit about planets and planetary correspondences in this book, and this activity showcases how you can use that information to create customized spells.

For this, I'm going to be adapting information from a grimoire called the Hygromanteia. This particular book deals a lot with angels, planets, and magic involving both. Notice how I used the word *adapting*. This might be your first time trying out magic this old, so I don't want to confuse you or bog you down with too much information. What I do want is for you to get a taste for what working with this kind of magic can feel like.

In the grimoires, plants, animals, rocks, and planets are all said to have their own "intelligences," with magic acting as a way of bringing that intelligence into one's own life. The word *intelligence* can be taken in a lot of different ways—you might read it as "spirit," "soul," "energy," or simply "vibes." However you choose to interpret intelligences, there are several reasons why you might want to call them into your life. Perhaps you need the communication skills and cleverness of Mercury or the boundaries and security of Saturn. Each planet has colors, metals, symbols, angels, and days of the week to bring these energies into your life. In the next chapter, we'll look at some charts that break this down further.

For now, if you don't know where to start or don't feel like you have a spe-cific need that requires magical assistance, consider looking up the day you were born and making a candle based on that.

For this activity, we are going to keep it simple and focus on a candle spell for Venus. However, if you have a copy of the Hygromanteia and would like to use this formula for a different planet, then absolutely feel free to do so. I like using Venus as an introductory planet because she rules over things that pretty much everyone needs and likes: love, money, and warm feelings—who couldn't use some of that? In the Hygromanteia, it is said that you should do magic on

a Friday (Venus's Day) for "operations towards marriage or connection of men in friendship or towards calling them wherever they may be to a place for kindness." So consider also using this spell for strengthening marriages, friendships, and kindness between people.

For this operation, you will need:

A green candle, large enough for you to carve symbols into

A spoon, chopstick, butter knife, or other tool for carving wax

Incense. The Hygromanteia calls for mastic resin for Venus work, which you can find at many health food stores. However, if that is unattainable, burning rose or musk incense works as well.

Optional items:

A copper plate. Copper is ruled by Venus and useful in Venus work. You can usually find cheap ones at thrift stores.

Themed music. This is not a very traditional suggestion, but when doing planetary work, I like to play music that makes me think of the planet I'm working with. This can be anything from the orphic hymns or the music of the spheres, to "God Is a Woman" by Ariana Grande. Remember, magic can be fun.

For this operation, you want to start on the day and hour of Venus, or, in normie speak, Friday at 1 a.m., 8 a.m., 3 p.m., or 10 p.m. There are free calculators online for helping determine planetary hours if this gets confusing.

Set up a small altar or clear a space on your existing altar for this ritual. If you are using a copper plate as a safe place to burn your candle, go ahead and put that on your altar.

Light your incense and take a moment to center yourself. Return to the breathing exercises from the first chapter and take a minute to reflect on what you want to channel with this planetary work.

Once you've centered yourself, take the candle and pass it through the smoke of the incense you are burning. If you want to play music during your ritual, start it now.

After you've fumigated the candle, take a dull but somewhat pointed object like a butter knife or chopstick and carve the symbol below into your candle:

SEAL OF VENUS

If you are performing this operation during Taurus or Libra season (when the Sun is in those signs), consider carving this symbol on the other side of the candle:

SEAL OF ANAEL

This is the seal of the angel Anael, who is associated with Venus.

Once you have your candle carved, hold it in your hands, and chant the following incantation:

"I conjure and declare and seal upon you, you strong and holy and powerful angels, in the name Hay, Hey, Hea, Ya, A, Ya, Ya, Ananey, in the name Saday, who created the beasts, reptiles, and men on the sixth day, and gave Adam power over all animals, thus may the name of the Creator be blessed in His place, and by the names of the angels who serve in the sixth host under Daghyel, the great angelic prince, strong and powerful, and by the name of the star that is Venus and her seal, since such a seal is sacred, and by all that has been said, I conjure upon you, the great angel Anael, who is the commander of the sixth day, that you work for me, [If you have a specific request, make it here]."

Light the candle and let it burn out.

Now, if you can't leave your candle until it burns all the way out—leaving a flame unattended is a bad idea in general—there are a few things you can do. I know some might disagree with this, but it has worked for me so feel free to give it a try. Make sure you burn your candle long enough so that it leaves an even burn pool and melts down. If you have to leave, blow the candle out and come back later to finish burning it. Try to time this so that when your candle burns out, it is at the same planetary day and hour on which you started. Repeat the conjuration you used earlier as thanks and discard any remaining wax at a crossroad.

FURTHER READING

Aside from the books mentioned earlier, there are some really excellent books and other sources to read if you want to know more about the history and practice of grimoires.

The Digital Ambler Blog, Sam Block

Sam Block is not only a wonderful person, but a great researcher and scholar as well. His blog is an invaluable resource for people studying magic, especially magic relating to the grimoires. The Digital Ambler was a great help to me while writing this book, and I can't recommend it enough.

Goetic Liturgy, Jake Stratton-Kent

Jake Stratton-Kent is one of the foremost scholars and practitioners of grimoire magic today. I could recommend any of his books here, but this one is particularly worth checking out if you would like grimoire magic to inform a deeper spiritual or religious pagan practice.

Grimoires, Owen Davies

One of the best books on occult history, this ends up being a great book on history in general. If you want to learn more about the history of grimoires and magic overall, this book should be on your bookshelf.

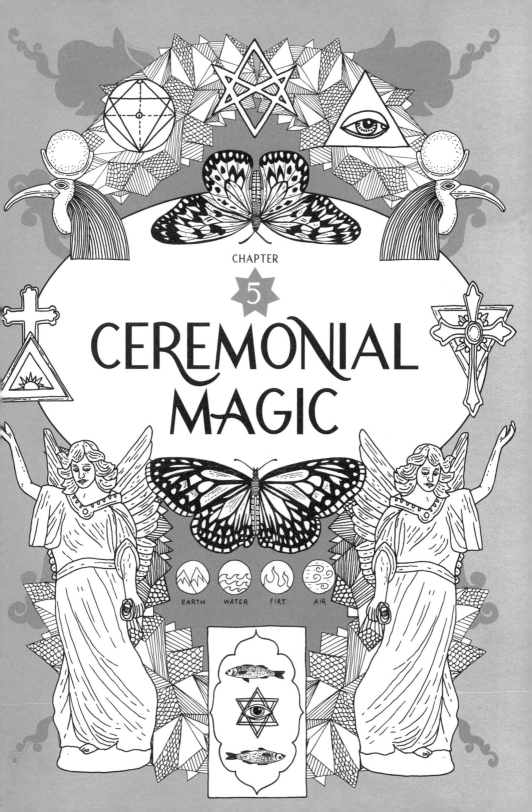

CHAPTER

5

CEREMONIAL MAGIC

EARTH   WATER   FIRE   AIR

I f you've ever seen a horror movie where figures in dark robes chant mysteriously, an anime where a character performs magic from the center of a glowing circle, or a show about uncovering secret societies, you've seen a reference to ceremonial magic. The aesthetics of this type of magic are so ubiquitous in pop culture that it's sometimes hard to tease out exactly *what* people are referencing.

Ceremonial magic is a broad term for mostly European magic that arose out of the grimoires and both Christian and Jewish mysticism. It's generally more standardized than witchcraft or chaos magic and places a great emphasis on study, discipline, and learning with a group of other magicians. Ceremonial magic is usually confusing and complex and often involves learning incredibly ornate rituals in order to perform magic. For this reason, it's also sometimes called ritual magic.

For a while—and sometimes still to this day—you would have heard people refer to the ideas in this chapter as simply "magic" and treat them as part of magic as a whole. I don't really have a problem with this when discussing European and Middle Eastern magic, since these ideas make up a large part of magical history in those regions. However, as I'm sure you can tell from this book, there are so many types of magic beyond just those traditions, and I think using the umbrella of ceremonial magic makes it a little more specific, at least for now.

In this chapter, we'll be looking at some of the different strains, religions, and groups that make up ceremonial magic.

HISTORY

Similar to grimoire magic, there is a lot of assumed knowledge when it comes to ceremonial magic. When you pick up a book on the subject or read blog posts about it, there's a whole vocabulary and history that most people expect you to know. I would understand this, if there were as many introductory books on Thelema and Hermeticism as there are on witchcraft and crystals, but this simply isn't the case.

Something I've struggled with over the years, and have seen other people struggle with, is putting ceremonial magic (and magic in general) into a historical context. Since so many practices feed off each other and the history of them sometimes goes back thousands of years, it can be difficult to know where people got certain ideas from. It can sometimes feel like you have to untie a knot of historical and magical terms and stories just to read a page of any book on ceremonial magic. To be frank, I find it very frustrating.

So I am going to give you the thing I wish I had had when I started studying magic, to hopefully help you avoid years of headaches. The following is a timeline of terms, groups, people, and ideas that make up the history of ceremonial magic and a large part of Western magic as a whole. It is arranged as chronologically as possible, to show how these ideas have built, borrowed, stolen, and enriched each other. This will (hopefully) streamline things and help you make sense of the words that get thrown around the magical world.

HERMETICISM (FIRST CENTURY)

I'll admit, it was difficult for me to choose where to talk about this in this book, mostly because Hermeticism is a philosophy that has influenced many types of magic over the centuries. I'm including it here because ceremonial magic is the style of magic it probably had the biggest impact on, but remember that Hermeticism's influence stretches far and wide.

Hermeticism is a Hellenic philosophy most likely dating to the first century CE. It was partially a reaction against Platonic philosophy, blending magical traditions from Greece and Egypt. Adherents of Hermeticism seek enlightenment through the achievement of something called *gnosis* and use magic, alchemy, and astrology to get there. The name Hermeticism comes from the mythic figure Hermes Trismegistus, a combination of the gods Hermes and Thoth, who legend says wrote some of the first books on magic.

The followers of this philosophy, who claimed that Hermes Trismegistus was writing through them, penned these early books—the collected twenty volumes of which are called the *Hermetica*. Hermeticism is a fairly broad term for a philosophy that has been around for centuries and therefore can't be pinned down too easily. However, there are some basic ideas that are found in most Hermetic texts:

THE MAGICIAN

"As above, so below."

This phrase appears in the Emerald Tablet, an eighth or ninth century alchemical Hermetic text. If Hermeticism has a key phrase, it's this. The idea is that anything that happens in the heavens has a resonance on the material plane. Essentially, it boils down to the concept that thoughts impact reality. This includes astrology, correspondences, and the cosmic rules of nature. The Magician card in the Rider-Waite-Smith tarot deck is a popular image that illustrates this concept.

Take some time to think about this phrase. Observe nature and see how different patterns repeat in big and small things, like how the branches of a tree, a lightning bolt, and the veins in your wrist all look similar. Choose an element or planet and see how its qualities manifest in different areas of life. How do ideas, thoughts, and "higher" concepts create reality in your life?

The Four Elements

Hermeticism uses the classical Greek elements as a foundation for a magical understanding of the universe. Earth, Water, Air, and Fire are cosmic building blocks to be studied and meditated upon. The four elements have been synchronized with many different things in magic over the years, from colors to directions to zodiac signs. Here is a short list of correspondences:

EARTH Cold and dry, north, green, Taurus, Virgo, Capricorn	**AIR** Hot and wet, east, yellow, Gemini, Libra, Aquarius	**FIRE** Hot and dry, south, red, Aries, Leo, Sagittarius	**WATER** Cold and wet, west, blue, Cancer, Scorpio, Pisces

The Seven Planets

The seven classical planets (Sun, Moon, Mercury, Venus, Mars, Jupiter, Saturn) are seen as forces that influence reality (as above, so below) and are also viewed as steps used in meditation to achieve gnosis. We say "classical" because other planets have been discovered in the last few centuries, and while these planets (Uranus, Neptune, Pluto) have begun to receive attention in magic and astrology, there just isn't as much lore or magical practice associated with them. (And yes, modern astrology still sees Pluto as a planet.)

Doing planetary magic and incorporating the wisdom of the planets into everyday life is a core component of Hermeticism, and understanding them will go a long way in helping you study magic. Below is a short correspondence list for the seven classical planets.

☉	☽	☿	♀
SUN Sunday, gold (color), Leo, gold (metal)	**MOON** Monday, silver (color), Cancer, silver (metal)	**MERCURY** Wednesday, orange, Virgo and Gemini, quicksilver	**VENUS** Friday, green, Taurus and Libra, copper

♂	♃	♄
MARS Tuesday, red, Aries and Scorpio, iron	**JUPITER** Thursday, purple, Sagittarius and Pisces, tin	**SATURN** Saturday, black, Aquarius and Capricorn, lead

Gnosis

While the word comes from the earlier philosophy of Gnosticism, the idea of gnosis is very important in Hermeticism and the occult orders it would influence.

Gnosis is similar to the idea of enlightenment or a state of grace. It refers to coming into a divine understanding or insight about the nature of the universe. This goes beyond an aha moment of sudden understanding—rather it's a deep understanding that brings one closer to divinity. Ideally, you want to have so many moments of gnosis that it leads to a permanent state of oneness, but this is rarely achieved.

Theurgy

Theurgy is essentially another way to say high magic or right-hand path magic. It is magic done for the achievement of gnosis and a "higher" purpose, as opposed to things like Goetia, where demons are summoned up for "lower" purposes like finding treasure or learning whom you'll marry.

Hermeticism would influence thinkers from the ancient world all the way up to Isaac Newton and beyond.

A book in 1908 called the *Kybalion* claimed authorship by the "Three Initiates" of Hermes Trismegistus, but it was likely written by a single individual. That book claims there are seven central teachings of Hermeticism, when in reality Hermeticism never had principles clearly defined in that way. I say this because you will likely run into this book at some point in your studies and I don't want you to get confused. This is a modern book that has influenced the New Age movement greatly, but not so much the occult world.

THE MIDDLE AGES

One misconception about magic is that it's an inherently pagan thing. In fact, beginning in the Middle Ages and up to the present day, people of all sorts of religions have worked with magic and incorporated elements from their own spirituality into its practice. Judaism, Christianity, and Islam all have rich magical traditions and practices that were formed or expanded on during the medieval period. We're going to look at two major developments.

THE KABBALAH (TWELFTH CENTURY)

Kabbalah (or Qabalah, or Cabala, or Kabbala—there are a few different spellings) is, in short, a form of Jewish mysticism, and, in not-so-short, is one of the major underpinnings of Western magic.

The name comes from the Hebrew root *kabel* which means "receive" and is sometimes interpreted as "oral tradition." While Judaism has a long history of mysticism and magic, Kabbalah developed in Southern Europe, specifically Spain and France, in the twelfth and thirteenth centuries. Around this time, two influential books—Sepher La-Bahir "The Book of Brilliance" and Sepher ha-Zohar "The Book of Splendor"—were published. Like the grimoires, the Zohar claims to have been written at an earlier time. These key works defined this strain of mysticism. Like almost every other book we will talk about in the history of magic, these volumes claimed earlier authorship and that they handed down ancient wisdom. Unlike most of these other books, however, there's probably some truth to this, with Kabbalah likely drawing on earlier Jewish traditions. Mysticism in Judaism goes back as far as the Book of Ezekiel, written around 593 BCE.

There are technically three different types of Kabbalah: Jewish Kabbalah, Christian Cabala, and Hermetic Qabalah. The timeline of this development goes something like this:

TWELFTH CENTURY—The first Jewish Kabbalistic texts are written in Spain.

FIFTEENTH CENTURY—Christian Cabala is created by Pico della Mirandola, who believed the Kabbalah to be a synthesis of ancient wisdom and proof that all mystical teachings eventually led to those of Christ.

SIXTEENTH CENTURY—Qabalah is formally synthesized with Hermeticism and magic in Cornelius Agrippa's (remember him?) landmark work *Occult Philosophy*.

Like I alluded to above, there are different spellings of the word *Kabbalah*, with three main variants. A basic rule of thumb is this: Kabbalah with a *k* is Jewish, Qabalah with a *q* is Hermetic, and Cabala with a *c* is Christian—and sometimes these are all spelled with a single or a double *b* and final *h*. For this book, when referring to Kabbalah broadly, I will use the Jewish spelling.

The Kabbalah is an incredibly deep philosophy and practice all on its own. For now, though, I'm just going to talk about the parts that pop up the most in magical studies.

The central motif of Kabbalah is the Tree of Life. Many rituals and concepts in ceremonial magic draw on this motif, so it's important to have a basic grasp of the idea. The Tree of Life is the same tree that grew in the Garden of Eden, and the ten spheres, or *sephiroth,* within it are emanations of God's creative power. There are twenty-two pathways that connect these sephiroth, each represented by one letter in the Hebrew alphabet, which also have numerical values. In Hermetic Qabalah, each pathway and sephiroth also corresponds to an element, planet, or sign of the zodiac. In meditation and ritual, you climb this tree to better understand God and achieve gnosis.

The Kabbalistic Tree of Life is a map of the cosmos, a human being, and the mind of God all at once (as above, so below). Following this map allows you to know yourself better. By knowing yourself better, you understand God better. Since God created humans in his own image, the idea is that by understanding God better, you understand the world better, yourself better, and so forth.

In the nineteenth century, a man who called himself Eliphas Levi synchro-nized Kabbalah with the tarot, which was later adopted by other magicians at

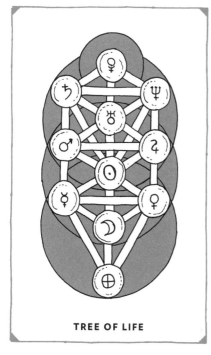

TREE OF LIFE

the time (see: The Golden Dawn and Aleister Crowley). It should be noted, though, that this was a historically recent development, and you can choose to use these correspondences or not in your own practice.

Now, let's back up a bit. What I just gave you is a *very* basic rundown of what Kabbalah is—but why are we talking about it at all? Well, in short, I think it's important that you know about it so you can decide whether you want to interact with it at all.

There are some who will claim that Kabbalah is something only Jewish people can practice. There are others who claim that you must understand and use Kabbalah if you are going to participate in the Western magical tradition at all. So, you might be wondering, am I willing to stake my claim/reputation on who is right here?

Here's the deal: Kabbalah was stolen from Spanish Jews and deliberately misinterpreted. It wasn't willingly shared, and the spread of Kabbalah is in part based on the violent expulsion of Jews from Spain in 1492. The thing—what we might think of as current, Hermetic Qabalah—that was formed from this theft bears very little resemblance to the original Kabbalah. When people say that you have to practice Qabalah to be a magician, that's simply not true. Whether you are dealing with grimoire magic, witchcraft, or even your own interpretation of ceremonial magic, this is not a model that everyone uses. If the appropriative roots of this practice make you uncomfortable or if it simply doesn't speak to you, don't feel pressured into incorporating Qabalah into your magical practice.

However, for about six hundred years, Hermetic Qabalah has been its own thing. We can have a debate about whether it should exist at all, but it does, and while I wouldn't say it forms the basis for all magic, for some systems it's important to at least understand, even if just for historical context. I would also add that most people who practice Kabbalah today, Jewish or otherwise, aren't men over the age of forty with children—the traditional requirements you're supposed to meet to study it.

When deciding how you'd like to interact with Kabbalah, I encourage you to think back to the chaos magic chapter for a bit. If Kabbalah is a magical model that works for you, then use it. If it speaks to you, moves you, or connects you to God, then I can't stand in the way of that.

Now, after vibing with a thing that works for you, come back and remember context. We can't take Kabbalah out of the history of magic or make it not work for us when it does, but we can act justly when we use it if we aren't Jewish. Try to buy books from Jewish scholars or learn about Jewish history as you study. We might come to magic as individuals, but we live our lives interconnected with other people. If our magical practices bring us to a deeper understanding of other people and leads us to help heal wounds of the past, then I think that can be a beautiful thing.

ENOCHIAN MAGIC (1583)

Enochian magic is a form of magic created by Queen Elizabeth I's magician John Dee. The name comes from the Book of Enoch, a supposed lost book of the Bible that tells the story of how angels came down from heaven and married mortal women. Dee was said to have made contact with angels in his workings and deciphered their language, called Enochian. Dee didn't call this form of magic Enochian (he just called it "angelic")—that came later with the Golden Dawn (more on them in a bit).

Similar to Hermetic Qabalah, Enochian magic is about moving up certain keys, or *aethyrs,* in order to make contact with angels at higher and higher stages of being. Just like levels in a video game, the aethyrs become harder to unlock as you go up the ladder. There are thirty aethyrs, each with three governors that guard them.

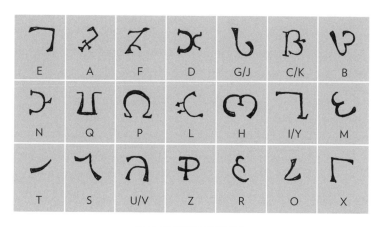

ENOCHIAN LETTERS

There are very few systems of magic I'll caution you against practicing in this book, but Enochian magic might be the exception. It's really, really not a beginner-friendly form of magic, and it's not that much friendlier to seasoned practitioners! I've seen Enochian magic really mess with people's mental health, especially if you don't have good ways to protect or ground yourself. It's said that even the great magician Aleister Crowley fell prey to the dangers of Enochian magic and it took a considerable toll on his mind and body. I don't know if the correct word to use is *ironic* when describing the fact that talking to angels for extended periods of time can make you lose your mind, but it's certainly not fun!

This doesn't mean to back away from angels entirely—we'll actually be incorporating angels in a ritual later—and it doesn't even mean that you should never research or practice Enochian magic. All I'm saying is that I wouldn't recommend you try to fly a plane after reading a book about automobile history.

So why am I even mentioning this Very Dangerous Form of Magic? Well, it's going to come up for you in your studies, and because so many magical paths are blended together, you might feel like this is something you have to learn in order to do Kabbalah, Hermeticism, witchcraft, or any number of other things. I'm here to say you don't and that you can work with angels without feeling the pressure to work through thirty aethyrs and pick up a drug habit along the way.

THE NINETEENTH CENTURY

As I'm sure you've noticed already, the nineteenth century saw an explosion of interest in magic. In a lot of ways, we are still living in the shadow of the ideas, movements, and religions that began during this time. This—like a lot of things we are still living with from the nineteenth century—is a mixed bag, but that's a subject for another book.

In magical books, it's often treated like a given that you already know who all the people and players of the nineteenth century are. Even if explanations are given, it can be hard to discern who was a member of what, which idea borrowed from which other idea, and what we're even talking about at all.

Some of this is due to the way these societies and people operated. Secret societies and social clubs were big in the nineteenth century, and people were normally members of more than one club—this goes for dinner clubs and occult orders alike. What happened at these meetings isn't always known (secret societies have a way of being secret), and sometimes people would copy what another group was doing without telling them. At the same time, most of these groups claimed they were recreating ancient religions or were passing on knowledge that had been handed down all the way from mythical societies like Atlantis—or Lemuria, if you're a Victorian hipster. This all makes it difficult to pinpoint when certain ideas came about. Think of this time period like a music scene, with all the creativity, passion, and drama that goes with it.

That said, I've still found it frustrating that it's only in history books, and not specifically occult books, that a sketch of this time is even attempted. I don't think you always have to know where a ritual or idea comes from for it to work, and I don't think you have to know every inch of occult history to be a "real" occultist, but I do think obscuring this time period is a way of gatekeeping this type of magic and, pardon my French, but I think that's lame.

To remedy that, here is a timeline of nineteenth-century ceremonial magic and occultism and a breakdown of the characters within it.

THE ROSICRUCIANS (1614)

Like the Freemasons (whom we'll discuss in a moment), the Rosicrucians technically began earlier than the nineteenth century, but I'm putting them in this part of the chapter because you mostly need to know about their impact on nineteenth-century occultism.

I don't want to spend too much time on these guys because, at the risk of being mean, I find them kind of boring. However, you will undoubtedly see them pop up if you study any

ROSICRUCIANS LOGO

sort of nineteenth-century magic, so it's good to be aware of them, even if just to know what not to pay much attention to.

It's tough to pinpoint exactly when the Rosicrucians began as an organization. We know that there were a series of pamphlets published in the early 1600s that alleged the existence of a secret, ancient organization called the Rosicrucians. These people were said to be secret wizards who studied alchemy, Hermeticism, and science and influenced the world from behind the scenes. Over four hundred pamphlets were published about this group. However, it is almost 1,000 percent certain that this organization was completely made up. Europe was a chaotic and scary place in the seventeenth century, though, and the notion of a secret order of benevolent wizards was very appealing to people.

Because this idea was so exciting, people started to make the Rosicrucians a reality, kind of like how people started setting up secret vampire societies after Anne Rice books became popular in the 1980s and '90s.

Rosicrucians use the language and tools of alchemy as metaphors for spiritual concepts. Their primary belief system can be seen as a blend of Hermeticism and Christianity. They would go on to influence Freemasonry's ideas around initiation and ritual. Offshoots and orders within the Rosicrucians continue today, with some of the latest orders being created as recently as the 1980s.

THE FREEMASONS (1717)

FREEMASONS LOGO

If you're an American reading this book, you probably know the Freemasons (or just the Masons) as that weird club most of the founding fathers were in and the inspiration for at least one Nicolas Cage movie. If you're not an American reading this book, I'm quite frankly not really sure what you were raised to believe about them! Apologies, but they don't teach us that other countries exist until about tenth grade in the United States.

In the Middle Ages in Europe, crafts and trades were structured around guilds. Guilds were groups you would join to learn skills of the craft, apprentice with seasoned workers, and climb through the ranks based on skill level and years in the organization. These guilds existed for things like carpentry, metalworking, and masonry.

While Freemason lore says the organization goes all the way back to one of these guilds, and even further to the mason Hiram, who built Solomon's Temple, the first Masonic Grand Lodge was founded in 1717 in London.

Freemasonry spread quickly and remains one of the most popular and mainstream occult orders in the world. Because they allowed men of all social rank into the order, it was considered fairly radical for its time. And since many of the heroes who came out of the American and French Revolutions were Masons, many conspiracy theories have sprung up around them. The Nazis stated that Freemasonry was one of the great enemies of the Third Reich, and if you scroll through YouTube long enough, you'll find some . . . let's say "interesting" opinions on the Masons. When people ask my political affiliation, I sometimes jokingly say I'm a member of the Anti-Masonic Party, despite having many lovely Mason friends, just because I think it's wild that a political party with that name really existed!

Freemasonry contains a complex language of symbols, a rite of initiation, and a system of ranks that went on to inspire future occult orders (and

Mormonism—again, another book). All the people and organizations we'll talk about were inspired by Freemasonry in one way or another.

In Freemasonry a new member, or initiate, is brought into the temple blindfolded before reenacting a symbolic death and rebirth. For each of the three degrees you ascend in Freemasonry, you undergo another ritual. Each level is modeled after the building of Solomon's Temple, and a Mason is expected to study the meanings behind the seemingly mundane symbols of that guild—the cable tow, the square, the compass—in order to progress up the ranks. You'll see these rituals and this structure reflected in Wicca, Thelema, and many other occult orders that were formed after the Masons.

HELENA BLAVATSKY (1831–1891)

A figure whose impact on history is greater than most history books would have you believe, Helena Blavatsky was born on August 12, 1831, in what is now Ukraine, to a wealthy family. She was a rebellious woman from a young age, rejecting the conventions and institutions women were forced into at the time and blazing her own path with a spiritual fortitude few possess. In her life, she would publish two books—*Isis Unveiled* and *The Secret Doctrine*—which would shake the spiritual core of Europe and the United States.

Blavatsky created a philosophy (movement? religion? honestly, it's hard to tell) called *Theosophy*. Put simply, Theosophy holds that all religions come from the same root, a secret religion that prevails over all things, and only some have ascended to true knowing. Theosophy is sort of like a spiritual secret society. She claimed to have been taught about this secret doctrine by members of this group she called "the ascended masters."

If you've heard about Blavatsky before, it's likely because she gets name-dropped a lot on

THEOSOPHICAL SOCIETY LOGO

documentaries about Nazis and the occult. It's true that her ideas about the "root races" of humanity went on to inspire some of history's worst villains, but it's also widely accepted by scholars that her ideas about race were naive, rather than malicious. You know that white girl who came back from a trip to India or Africa and now believes we're all connected through vibes or something? Blavatsky is the antecedent of that type of person. She basically thought of race like the Power Rangers or one of Captain Planet's Planeteers. In her view, which race you were gave you different powers and deficiencies. As I'm sure you can see, this is at best a pretty silly idea that in the wrong hands can be used for awful purposes. The most famous example of this occurred years after Blavatsky's death, when the Nazis created a spin-off movement known as Ariosophy, in which white people were the only ascended masters, or people with magical powers. The best defense scholars can mount for Blavatsky in the face of all this is that, in the same way she was foolish in her ideas around race and class, Blavatsky was a fool for not seeing how these ideas would be interpreted by those with malintent.

I have a hot take that Blavatsky is less an occult figure, and more a New Age one, since she wasn't drawing so much on grimoires, witchcraft, or alchemy, but on misinterpreted ideas about Hinduism and Buddhism. You see her ideas about a secret religion, hidden masters, and an attempt to unite with the oneness of creation pop up in yoga studios, New Age bookstores, and plastic surgeons' offices in Malibu without people even realizing they are basically following in her footsteps. Still, her reputation as an occultist is understandable, since Theosophy was very popular and influential and Blavatsky herself was said to perform miracles in her lifetime.

While Theosophy is still around, you don't meet many Theosophists today. I think its inability to maintain the hold on adherents that other occult religions have been able to is due in part to the absolutely dense, inscrutable, confusing nature of Blavatsky's writing, and also the fact that actual Hinduism and Buddhism are sitting right there—nowadays people will just go to the source and cut out the intermediary.

THE HERMETIC ORDER OF THE GOLDEN DAWN (1888)

We've finally arrived! Throughout this book, I've name-dropped this particular organization quite a bit. That's because the Hermetic Order of the Golden Dawn (the Golden Dawn for short) was one of the most, if not *the* most, influential magical groups in history, for better or worse.

HERMETIC ORDER OF THE GOLDEN DAWN LOGO

The Golden Dawn was founded in 1888 in London by three Freemasons: William Wynn Westcott, Samuel Liddell Mathers, and William Robert Woodman. The beginnings of the organization, while somewhat interesting, aren't as important as the structure and impact of this group—just know they involve a made-up German countess and fake secret societies. The founders also claimed they had been contacted by "The Secret Chiefs," a concept similar to bodhisattvas in Mahayana Buddhism, that comes from Victorian understandings of Sufism and Buddhism. Basically, Secret Chiefs are spiritual beings that provide help to magical seekers and maintain the secret hierarchy of the universe. These guys will be important later, so keep them in mind.

While the structure of the Golden Dawn was similar to that of the Freemasons, it differed in that women could join, and many first-wave feminists, radical thinkers, and artists became members. The organization of the group was based around previous Rosicrucian orders the founders had been in, as well as Hermetic Qabalah. Members were expected to climb up spiritual "grades" as their understanding and command of magic grew, with each grade relating to a different sphere on the Tree of Life. For some people, it was a very serious organization that was committed to discovering the secrets of the cosmos, while for others it was a fun club where you could meet and hang out with like-minded friends.

The organization chugged along happily for a few years, but as seems to be the case with all occult scenes, drama started tearing it apart. Without getting too in the weeds about it, remember those Secret Chiefs? Well, members of the Golden

Dawn began to grow suspicious about why founding member and then-current leader Samuel Mathers was the only person who got to talk to them. They felt he was either lying about the nature of these Chiefs or lying about the messages he was receiving from them—either way, many members thought he was taking the group in a bad direction. This resulted in a war with Mathers and Aleister Crowley on one side and William Butler Yeats (yes, that one) and other members on the opposite side. Eventually, this conflict would cause the group to dissolve.

While now obscure, it's hard to overstate the influence of the Golden Dawn at the time. If you have ever used the widely available Rider-Waite-Smith tarot card deck, you have touched a part of the legacy of the Golden Dawn. Arthur Edward Waite and Pamela Colman Smith were both members and designed the deck around their modern understanding of what the cards meant. (Rider is the name of the publisher.) This has influenced all of tarot, up through the present day and likely for as long as people will use tarot. Writers like Bram Stoker, Yeats, and Arthur Machen were members, in addition to occultists like Crowley, Dion Fortune, and Gerald Gardner, as well as many famous actors and artists of the day. The influence this group had on art, horror, literature, and magic is truly incalculable.

Our modern understanding of Qabalah has largely been formed by this organization too, as has people's very definition of what magic is—or at least was for more than a century. Before the Golden Dawn, magic was seen as an uncontrollable force, a natural phenomenon or way of looking at the world, like electricity. Under the influence of the Golden Dawn, magic became a field of study, a "science," and a unified, singular force that came from one place—Egypt, in their cosmology—and could be harnessed. In true Victorian fashion, they thought magic could be contained, studied, and bound, but unfortunately we need only look at similar ideas around gender, race, and empire that came out of this same era to see how limited this way of thinking is.

For a long time, people looked fairly uncritically at the Golden Dawn. They were big, they were influential, they changed magic, and that's all that mattered. However, more recently, people have been taking a different perspective and reassessing its importance.

While absolutely significant in the development and history of magic, the Golden Dawn's influence was arguably sometimes harmful, or at the very least distorting. Yes, you *can* link tarot to Qabalah, but it's not an essential part of the tool. Yes, their degrees of initiation and rituals *might* be the right fit for you, but you don't have to use them or link any sort of hierarchy to magical learning. Sure, ancient Egypt is great, and it's fine to be inspired by other cultures and religions— but is stealing and retooling ancient ideas and practices because "you know better" while your government is actively colonizing those countries, as the kids say, "a good look"? The Golden Dawn had a particular stance on magic—that it was ancient, unified, came from a singular source, and must be learned in a school-like setting—which was treated for about a century as fact, rather than opinion.

What do I keep saying in this book? If any ideas or rituals from the Golden Dawn work for you, then that's great, but it's also important to recognize their handprints on certain magical ideas and writings so you can sift through it. Their ideas are not givens, and much has changed since their time. I personally honor the legacy of the Golden Dawn and many of its members for paving the way for future occultists, but I leave most of their practices and ideologies out of my own spiritual life. They are important to know about, but not necessary to engage with.

ALEISTER CROWLEY (1875-1947)

Not a magical order, but a person—and a very important one at that—proto-edgelord Aleister Crowley probably had a bigger impact on magic in the modern period than any other individual. A bisexual, self-styled diabolist born into a wealthy, evangelical British family, Crowley found himself at odds with the world very quickly. Over the course of his life, he would travel the globe to learn the secrets of magic and in the process would not only create his own religion, but blow up and reform the occult world as we know it. For this, and many other reasons, Crowley remains a controversial figure.

Born into a wealthy religious family that owned the modern equivalent of a restaurant chain, Crowley followed his evangelist father around as he preached the word of God, drawn to the power of commanding a room with a sermon. After his father's early death, Crowley's interests turned away from Christianity. He began calling himself "The Great Beast 666" (see what I meant by proto-edgelord?) and became fascinated with the occult. After he graduated from college—sorry, *university*—he believed, as many people do when they start studying magic, that there must be a secret, ancient group of real magicians out there who would teach him the art of it. What Crowley ended up finding was the Golden Dawn.

Crowley was initiated into the Golden Dawn in 1898 and quickly rose through the ranks of the order, surpassing longtime members. He also just as quickly found himself at odds with many other members of the Golden Dawn, including famous Irish poet and artist W. B. Yeats. Some of this, I think, is understandable on Crowley's part. As I said earlier, the Golden Dawn was little more than a social club for a lot of people, and I can see how someone who wanted to do real magic might be disappointed and upset if he were essentially promised Narnia and ended up at Comic Con. Crowley was also bisexual or queer at a time when that was very much taboo, even among free-minded occultists. However, it must be remembered that Crowley was also a huge jerk—and that tends not to endear yourself to others. As we already covered, at this time there was a schism forming in the Golden Dawn, with Mathers and Crowley on one side and a good portion of the rest of the order on the other. This opposition objected to the way Mathers was running things and claimed he was too controlling (for what it's worth, I think this criticism was probably right).

This schism eventually tore the Golden Dawn apart, and after a magical war (yes, really) Crowley was exiled from the order. Bitter but as dedicated to magic as ever, Crowley went on to forge his own path, even as he took the format of his future orders from the Golden Dawn. We'll cover those in a bit.

When you first get into magic, there are going to be lots of people who tell you that Crowley is the be-all and end-all of magic, and there might even be some people who make you feel dumb for not knowing everything about the man. Some of this praise is understandable—he is a prophet to a lot of people, after all—and Crowley absolutely changed not only the world of magic, but the world as a whole. A modern evangelist for the practice of magic, Crowley wrote dozens of books, founded a religion, was (supposedly) a spy during World War I, and was one of the first modern celebrities, being dubbed "the wickedest man in the world" by the press. Crowley took formerly disparate magical disciplines from across Europe, the Middle East, and Asia and synthesized them under a unified theory of what magic is. There's a reason he appeared on a Beatles album cover, Alice Cooper wrote a song about him, Jay-Z wore a sweatshirt quoting him, and Led Zeppelin's Jimmy Page went so far as to buy his former home. Crowley made the occult rock-and-roll.

That said, Aleister Crowley is a complex figure who I think many people wish were simple. As you study magic, you're going to encounter a lot of strong feelings about this man in every direction. Some people think he's entirely over-rated, a relic of the past, and an all-around bad person who should be discarded entirely. Others see him as the ultimate representation of what a magician can be—a daring figure who was far ahead of his time, carved his place into history, and liberated magic for the masses. For what it's worth, I think both sides are correct and wrong at the same time. Crowley was a self-centered jerk who left a trail of discarded lovers and neglected children in his wake. He was a wealthy man living in the imperial core of Victorian England and embodied many of the problems and ideas that came from being in his social class. He was also the first person to begin breaking ceremonial magic out of its lofty tower and was the first to define magic as a force that anyone, from any class, can and should seize for their liberation. Crowley is not a figure who can be discounted, but he isn't a person you have to admire either.

Like the Beatles, while you have to know about Crowley, you don't have to like him. I think it's important to understand his impact so you can choose whether you want to engage with him or not. Certain ideas we take for granted in magic studies come from him—the journal prompt in this book is a Crowley thing—and I'm sure you've seen in the preceding chapters that his name pops up a lot. However, in the last few years there has been a move away from not only Crowley, but the nineteenth century's influence on magic as a whole, as magical practitioners rekindle an interest in folk magic, the grimoires, and African Diasporic Religions. Crowley is important because he made himself important, but if you want to simply know about him as a historical figure and then move on, that's okay.

With all that in mind, let's look at some of the things Crowley was directly involved in creating. He can be credited with laying the early seeds of both chaos magic and Wicca, but for now here are the organizations he established or helped lead.

Thelema (1904)

Thelema is a magical philosophy and belief system founded by Aleister Crowley and still followed by thousands of people all over the world. It is often called a religion, and while that is not inaccurate, it's a little bit more accurate to say that Thelema is a spiritual path and philosophy. Thelema's central message is that you have not only the right, but the moral imperative, to determine your divine place in the cosmos and then live it to the fullest, the social mores of your age be damned.

While its official date of creation is 1904, the religion wouldn't standardize until later in Crowley's life. In 1904 Crowley and his then-wife Rose were sleeping in the Great Pyramid of Giza (because you could do that back then) when Rose began to channel a message from the Egyptian god Horus. After

UNICURSAL
HEXAGRAM

questioning her about this revelation, Crowley became convinced she had indeed made contact and he needed to open himself up to whatever message would come through.

Over the next three days, Crowley made contact with a being named Aiwass and summoned this being over and over again, writing down what they said. At the end of the three days, he had transcribed what would go on to become *The Book of the Law* or *Liber AL vel Legis*. This is the central text of Thelema and, in my opinion, a great read. It tells us that humans have been through two ages—the age of Isis dominated by goddess religions and the age of Osiris dominated by patriarchy. It goes on to say that we will soon enter into the age of Horus the child—the age we are currently in—which will be filled with both freedoms and horrors previously unthinkable. In this age, magic and the doctrine of Thelema, it is said, will be the dominant worldview.

The word *thelema* comes from the Greek word "will," and the goal of Thelema, and arguably all of Crowley's teachings, is to find your "true will" and live by it. *Will* itself is a complicated idea and something you can spend a lifetime understanding. A lot of people think the central tenet of Thelema, "Do what thou wilt shall be the whole of the law," means "do whatever you want," but this is a pretty simplistic take.

Your Will in this context is something like the idea of destiny, the thing you are supposed to embody in this life and live in accordance with to achieve harmony with the cosmos and everyone in it. Have you ever just known you had to live your life a certain way or take a certain risk and, after doing so, felt like you just had an incredible sense of luck and direction? Thelemites would say this is you living your Will, and that ease is you aligning yourself with a divine order. Crowley really believed that if people "followed their heart," so to speak, we would live in a better world, because discord comes from repression. Think about this from the perspective of someone who was bisexual in the nineteenth century. By following his Will and openly expressing his sexuality, Crowley was going against the moral decree of his time, but he was also probably happier and more harmonized than if he had repressed his Will. As with any religion, there are many people who take the law of Thelema as a free pass to be absolute assholes to everyone around them, but it is by no means a forgone conclusion that being a Thelemite makes you a bad person.

The second part of the law of Thelema often gets cut out when it is being quoted, but the full line is: "Do what thou wilt shall be the whole of the law, love is the law, love under Will." Some people take this to mean "do what you want, and damn everyone else," while others interpret it to mean something along the lines of "follow your true self, so long as you are guided by love." To be a Thelemite, all one has to do is follow this code (and maybe read *The Book of the Law* from time to time), but there is no formal rule beyond that. However, if you want to formalize your practice, there are two major magical orders that are set up to do just that.

The A∴A∴ (1907)

A∴A∴ LOGO

The A∴A∴ was Crowley's first attempt to formalize his ideas of magic into a linear process. The A∴A∴ isn't really a club or lodge like the Masons. Instead, it's very secretive, and even if you are in the A∴A∴, you don't know who the other members are.

The A∴A∴ is set up along the Golden Dawn's grade system, where one is expected to climb to higher states of consciousness based off the Kabbalistic Tree of Life. When you join the A∴A∴, you are basically assigned a teacher from a higher grade who is there to help you out on your magical journey. This person doesn't sit you down and walk you through how to do magic, but instead acts as a resource whom you can ask questions of and get advice from.

The symbol of the A∴A∴ is the seal of Babalon, the goddess of love and war who represents a state in Crowley's magical system that is similar to ego death. Once achieving power, you must give yourself over to her in order to be cleansed of the ego, or else you risk being overwhelmed by malignant forces in the universe. Believe it or not . . . no one really knows what "A∴A∴" stands for! After Crowley died, different lineages of the A∴A∴ began to form—similar to Wicca—that all claim different meanings for the abbreviation, but ask seven Thelemites what it means and you'll get 777 different answers.

The A∴A∴ was Crowley's attempt to systematize finding true Will and create a formal path of initiation. However, it is not the only way to follow his teachings, and Crowley himself would urge you to forge your own path. If you do want to follow a formal path in Thelema, though, there's also another major group that follows his teachings, known as the OTO.

The OTO 1904, 1912*

OTO LOGO

The OTO (short for Ordo Templi Orientis) was a magical society that was technically formed in 1904 but was reformed into the order we know today in 1912. Let me explain.

When the OTO was first formed, it had very secret rituals based on sex magic and Eastern mysticism. In 1912, OTO founder Karl Kellner came across Crowley's writing, and the rituals of the A∴A∴, and thought he had stolen them from the OTO. Furious, he asked Crowley for a meeting, thinking he was going to call Crowley out for his thievery. However, when the two met and had a long conversation about the issue, Kellner realized that Crowley had never even heard of the OTO and had come to these conclusions on his own.

Believing this was proof that Crowley really was the greatest magician of the age, Kellner invited him to take over the OTO and transform it how he saw fit. So while the OTO was not originally formed by Crowley, it was reformed by him to embody his philosophy of magic.

The OTO is more akin to Masonic orders or other public magical groups than the A∴A∴. It's a social organization that places great emphasis on public ritual and dramatic performances, and decades after its creation, it would welcome musicians like David Bowie into its ranks.

There are two subsections within the OTO, and this is where Thelema-stuff can get a little alphabet soup-y, so stay with me. The EGC (Ecclesia Gnostica Catholica) administer mass and handle the basic rituals and running of the OTO, while the MMM (Mysteria Mystica Maxima) are more intense and meant to initiate people into, and be evangelists for, the religion. You do not have to be part of either subgroup to be in the OTO.

The rituals of the OTO are based around something called **the Gnostic Mass,** a dramatization of the *Book of the Law*. It is said you must embody a myth to truly understand it, and the Gnostic Mass is designed to do just this.

The Gnostic Mass is somewhat similar to the traditional Catholic mass, but it is ultimately a Thelemic ritual and meant to affirm Thelemic values, mythological ideas, and ethics. If you go to one, newcomers are encouraged to participate and receive communion, unlike a Catholic mass where one must be baptized into the religion in order to fully participate.

As I said, you don't need to join any of these orders to be a Thelemite, adhere to Crowley's idea of magic, or practice magic in general. However, if these ideas sound appealing to you and you want structure or a social component for your practice, then investigating them might be worth your while.

CEREMONIAL MAGIC TODAY

Okay, here's the deal.

Magic is an ancient and complex way of understanding the world. It's beautiful and deep and about exploring the ultimately unknowable mysteries of the universe. It's also extremely nerdy, and as a nerdy art, there are turf wars, with people insisting they have the "correct" magical system, thank you very much. Do you think that sounds silly? Wow, I bet you liked *The Last Jedi* too.

It's important for us to unpack this pretentiousness before we leave the world of ceremonial magic, because this attitude is what keeps a lot of people from studying it and it will undoubtedly be something you run into. Ceremonial magic is a broad term for Western occult practices that involve heavy ritual, have degrees of initiation, and often draw on medieval magic—with interpretations of Egyptian and Babylonian magic sometimes included as well. Because of the time it takes to study, and the fact that the books needed to study it were pretty expensive and hard to find until very recently, it is a form of magic historically practiced by wealthy white men.

For the past couple hundred years, this has been called "high magic," as opposed to "low magic." High magic is done for a "higher" purpose, like communing with angels for the fun of it or ascending to being a god on earth, while low magic is done for a "lower" purpose, like healing your sick cow or cursing the king who wants to come and take your land. You'll also see similar phrases like "left-hand" and "right-hand" path magic to describe a similar divide. Left-hand path magic is done for "selfish" or bad reasons, and right-hand path magic is done for "selfless" or holy reasons.

Do you see how class relations, misogyny, and racism are so baked into these terms? High magic is what rich dudes with time and money to spare do to fill their time, while low magic is what those silly witches and enslaved people do.

These terms are largely out of fashion today for these very—and very good—reasons. You'll see them pop up now and then, but in the past few decades there has been a shift to change "high magic" to "ceremonial magic" and "low magic" to terms like "folk magic" or "witchcraft."

You might be thinking, "well, if there's so much bad stuff in ceremonial magic, why talk about it at all?" That's a natural question, and there are a few answers. For one, I think there are some cool ideas and beautiful rituals in ceremonial magic, which will only be made better through adding more perspectives to the conversation. I think ceremonial magic needs to be opened up for its own sake. Ceremonial magic is all about discipline, study, and inner work. These are good things! I like these things! I just think they can be done without looking down your nose on everyone who isn't doing them.

The other reason is that ceremonial magic is central to the history of Western occultism, which you should know about if only to recognize its influence when starting your own practice. If you've ever cast a circle while doing witchcraft, for instance, you've done a ceremonial magic.

I once overheard a conversation at an occult bookstore that's useful to reflect on here. A young woman who was a beginner came in asking where to start. The person behind the counter insisted that she needed to read the works of Aleister Crowley and study ceremonial magic if she wanted to be "serious" about studying magic. It took all my strength not to scream "NO" at this shop clerk. As you study magic, people are likely to do the same thing to you. You will get messages, consciously or unconsciously, that ceremonial magic is "real" magic and the rest is just silly New Age crap.

The thing is, ceremonial magic is *complicated*. It's all purposefully written in erudite, obscure language to make it difficult for the noninitiated to study, and it has a nearly two-thousand-year history that is often built on other people's bad reading of even earlier history. While it's important to understand and I think can be a powerful practice for a lot of people, I really don't think diving into ceremonial magic headfirst, without any context, is the smartest move.

What I hope you've been able to see in this chapter is the influence this style of magic has had on magic as a whole. Perhaps even more important, I hope you can see both the shortcomings and appeal of this approach.

JOURNAL PROMPTS

- What role does structure play in my life? Does my spiritual practice require more or less structure?

- What does the phrase "as above, so below" evoke in me? What examples of this principle can I find throughout the day?

- What does the phrase "Do what thou wilt" mean to me? What comes up for me when I think about the full phrase: "Do what thou wilt shall be the whole of the law. Love is the Law, love under will"?

- Do I have a spiritual community? Do I feel the need to make or strengthen community in my life?

- What has happened in my life since trying out ceremonial magic? Has my life gotten better or worse?

- When I do these rituals, where do I feel them in my body? Do my mind and body feel united or disconnected?

- If I encountered beings or spirits during these rituals, what did they look, sound, or feel like?

THE LESSER BANISHING RITUAL
OF THE PENTAGRAM

Remember when I went into all that detail on Qabalah and said we would come back to it? Well, we're coming back to it!

To get a sense of what ceremonial magic feels like, we're going to go through the Lesser Banishing Ritual of the Pentagram, or LBRP for short. This was the ritual that neophytes, or newbies, had to learn when they first joined the Golden Dawn. It is also a cornerstone of the A∴A∴, OTO, and pretty much all ceremonial magic practiced today.

If I can share a #hottake for a moment, I think one of the big differences between ceremonial magic and something like chaos magic, for instance, is that ceremonial magic is very embodied. Magic lives in and flows through your body in ceremonial magic.

There's been a lot of research conducted in recent years on how trauma, stress, and emotional pain affect the body, sometimes for years. Trauma and negative emotions live in the body until they are moved through and processed and can often show up as chronic pain and sickness. That's one reason why I think the LBRP is such a cool ritual. Through chanting, visualization, and movement, it is designed to clear a space, purify yourself of negative energy, and strengthen and protect you against malevolent forces. In magical terms, it does this by mimicking the way God created reality and awakening the divine force in you. In material terms, it does this by clearing your head and allowing painful memories or events to move through you.

As Above, So Below.

Someday, I really hope someone will write a book combining somatic therapy with ceremonial magic (maybe it will be you!), but that is, unfortunately, not this book. For now, we're going to go through this ritual, and see how it makes us feel.

Now, before we go any further, I know that because of the Abrahamic influence on this ritual that some people might be uncomfortable performing it at

111

first. A main idea in ceremonial magic is that if God created us in his image, then we are like God and are thus able to shape reality through magic. It's safe to say this was the main theory behind how magic worked for several centuries. Nowadays though, people are used to applying different models of magic, like the psychological or cybernetic model, not to mention many people get into magic precisely to move *away* from Christianity and other Abrahamic religions.

I avoided ceremonial magic for years for this reason—the biblical influence threw me off—and I don't want to pressure you to do something you just don't want to do. But before you give up entirely, I ask that you go back and read over the chaos magic chapter a bit—there's a reason we talked about that one first. See if shifting the paradigm around the LBRP makes you feel more comfortable. Maybe instead of imagining yourself as an emanation of God, you see yourself as embodying the divine within you or channeling your inner power. Maybe put on the pointy Crowley hat for a bit and see how it fits. If all else fails, remember that David Bowie used to do this ritual each day and Kate Bush wrote a song about it. There's something to it.

The LBRP is both a cleansing and protective ritual. It is you pushing out negative influences from yourself and your space. It is also you declaring your power and saying "watch out" to malefic spirits and energies that might want to do you harm.

It is suggested that you do the LBRP twice a day. If you want to go all in, by all means do so, or for now try doing it once a day for a week and see how that feels. I usually do mine in the morning, but the evening is also fine.

The first step in the ritual is to make the Qabalistic Cross. This involves vibrating the Hebrew words for the Lord's Prayer as you visualize light flowing through your body. This is meant to embody the idea that the divine is not an outside force, but something dwelling within your body and that you are a reflection of the divine. You are announcing to the universe "I'm here, I'm divine, get used to it."

PART ONE

THE QABALISTIC CROSS

Stand facing east. If you cannot stand or have limited mobility, sit facing east and visualize through light whatever movements you can't make with your body.

Take a few deep breaths and relax into your body. Return to the breathing and meditation exercises in chapter 1 if you need to.

Above your head, visualize a beautiful white light. I like to also envision the stars and heavens above me. Gradually, let this light descend into the top of your head.

Raise your right hand and touch your index and middle finger to the center of your forehead. Visualize the light coming down and connecting with your hand.

Chant the word *Ateh* (ah-tah). When you do this, don't just say the word—chant it deep in your chest so it vibrates through your body. Let yourself *feel* these words.

The light strengthens in place as you move your hand down to the center of your chest.

Chant the word *Malkuth* (mal-kooth) in the same way. Let the light grow in your chest as the word vibrates throughout your body.

Move your hand to your right shoulder, drawing the light with it.

Chant the word *Vegeburah* (ve-gay-boo-ra).

Place your hand on your left shoulder. The light should now form a cross, with you in the center.

Chant the word *Vegedulah* (ve-ged-oo-la).

Place both your hands over your chest and visualize the light growing to encompass your whole body.

Chant the words *Le-Olahm, Amen* (le olam, ah-men).

What you are doing here is reciting the Lord's Prayer in Hebrew. Translated, it means the following:

Ateh—*Thou Art*
Malkuth—*The Kingdom*
Vegeburah—*The Power*

Vegedulah—*and the Glory*
Le-Olahm, Amen—*Forever and Ever, Amen*

PART TWO

THE PENTAGRAM

Now that you have called up your own divine power, you are going to chant the names of God and invoke the archangels to cleanse your space and create a circle of protection.

Still facing east, you will now start to make what's called the banishing pentagram of earth in the four directions. To do this, start at the bottom left, and swipe up in the air, like the diagram below:

As you make this symbol, visualize it glowing in front of you. You can use your hands or a wand to do this.

Still facing east, make the banishing pentagram above and chant **IHVH** (yea-ho-wah).

Turn south (moving clockwise), make the pentagram, and chant **ADNI** (Adonai).

Turn west, make the pentagram, and chant **AHIH** (Eh-he-ay).

Turn north, make the pentagram, and chant **AGLA** (Agla).

Turn back toward the east, stretch your arms out to either side, and say:

> *"Before me, Raphael,*
> *Behind me, Gabriel,*
> *On my right, Michael,*
> *On my left, Auriel.*
> *For about me flames the pentagram,*
> *and in the center stands the*
> *six-rayed star."*

Repeat the Qabalistic Cross from step one.

You can do this ritual before a magical working to protect yourself, like a standard magic circle. Or you might perform it once or twice a day to keep yourself cleansed and protected. I like to do this in the morning before I meditate, but try it out and see what works best for you.

After you do this ritual, take a minute to take stock of how the LBRP feels in your body. I normally feel calm and maybe a little light-headed afterward. Where did you feel the words you chanted? Could you feel your body change as you extended your energy outward? Ceremonial magic needs to be embodied to be understood, and how your body feels after doing this ritual for a few days or weeks might give you a clue as to how much you want to pursue ceremonial magic as a practice.

FURTHER READING

The Book of the Law, Aleister Crowley
If you only read one book by Crowley, let it be this. A beautiful and poetic book, even if you don't end up liking Crowley or practicing Thelema, it's hard not to be moved by this text.

High Magick, Damien Echols
Truly one of the simplest and most accessible books on ceremonial magic.

The Magick of Aleister Crowley, Lon Milo DuQuette
The secret to understanding Crowley is to read books about his magic before you actually read books of magic written by him. All of DuQuette's books are great and worth checking out, but this is a good place to start for simple ritual guides and straightforward answers about why you might do them.

CHAPTER

6

WITCHCRAFT

While writing this book, this chapter was, initially, the first thing I decided to work on. Eventually though, I put it aside and ended up writing it last. I think I did this because, even for a practicing witch, of all the many forms of magic witchcraft might be the hardest to define, trace, and categorize.

Witchcraft, and more broadly the concept of *the witch,* has meant many things to many people throughout history. It is a pact with the devil made at the crossroads. It is a heresy against God. It is the path walked by the descendants of Eve. It is the secret language of plants and shadows. It is the survival of an ancient goddess religion. It is a Halloween decoration. It is a feminist act of rebellion. It is something you can buy in a store. It is a crime.

Are all these statements true? Are none of them true? The witch cackles at an attempt to define them, to trap them into a neat little box, but in this chapter I will try to do just that. It is my opinion that witchcraft is all of the above and none of the above—that ambiguity is part of the fun. Witchcraft is a practice, to some it is a religion, and to many more it is a symbol. Beyond that, it is still a crime in many parts of the world and was in Europe and its colonies for centuries. Understanding what witchcraft *is* and how to do it means untangling these threads as best we can and following them through time.

Witchcraft has exploded in popularity in recent years. There's a good chance you picked up this book specifically for this chapter. The good news and bad news is that witchcraft is complicated, yet intuitive. It has been the repository for many magical traditions over time, picking up shiny things along the way, and as such it is a highly individualized form of magic. Ask two Thelemites, druids, or even chaos magicians to define their practice, and you'll likely get two similar answers. The same cannot usually be said of witchcraft. While this can cause some people out of very reasonable frustration to plant their flag firmly in the camp of one definition or another, I've finally chosen to embrace the ambiguity and love witchcraft for its weirdness.

In this chapter, I'm going to try to spell out a somewhat coherent history of witchcraft. I'm going to (spoiler alert) assert that there are four different major paths, or kinds of witchcraft, and I'm going to open the door to each path to see if any are intriguing to you. Overall, I hope that even if you choose not to become a witch, you'll walk away with a new appreciation for the craft. Few forms of magic have the grip on the imagination that witchcraft does, and I hope by the end of this chapter, you'll see why.

History

Over the years, I've tried to explain what witchcraft is to many people, only to have them move away with confused looks on their faces. It can really seem like witchcraft is everything you've been led to believe it is, and nothing like that at all.

What I've found works best is not to define a singular witchcraft, but to go through a history of witchcraft, or at least what has been called witchcraft, and let people decide for themselves which flavor they like best. If you'll allow me to get scholarly for a moment (and heck, I'm on my second book, so I think I'm allowed), it is my belief that there are four "witchcrafts" that correspond roughly to four different historical eras. They are:

◆ Ancient "shamanic" witches

◆ Cunning craft and wisepeople

◆ Pagan religious witchcraft

◆ Modern witchcraft

I want to say two things up front. First, this is how *I* best understand witchcraft, and aside from similar thoughts from Professor Ronald Hutton, I haven't seen it spelled out like this anywhere else. Feel free to disagree and disregard this. Second, it's completely possible to pull from each of these four strains of witchcraft, and I'd argue that most witches already do to some extent.

With all that in mind, let's dive into the history of witchcraft and learn its many definitions along the way.

ANCIENT HISTORY AND SHAMANIC WITCHCRAFT

Before we go any further, I want to quickly address the word *shaman*. While this word was originally only used by the Indigenous people of Siberia to describe individuals who could talk to spirits, go into trance states, and divine things like the cause of sickness in order to help their community, it was popularized by anthropologists and became the catchall term for people—usually Indigenous—who weren't really priests, but calling them wizards or witches felt icky and weird, with good reason.

Today there's a whole discipline of magic called Shamanism, and while even more nebulous than witchcraft, it usually involves drumming, trance states, animal and spirit guides, and the idea that the soul has many parts. While I know shamans who don't engage in gross appropriation of Indigenous practices and who are not only initiated into many magical traditions but are respectful of the ones they are not, this is unfortunately rare.

There is a debate around whether to drop the term *shamanism* altogether in magic. I agree with this wholeheartedly as it pertains to Indigenous people—we should call the people who keep their ceremonies and spiritual knowledge whatever they prefer to be called. But when it comes to the history of European magic, these words are deeply embedded in the history we're about to discuss (and, frankly, using *shaman* and *shamanism* is a lot simpler than me constantly writing out "spiritual practitioner and community healer who also served as town historian"). While we can all agree the term might be outdated, at best, I hope you'll be patient with me for now.

Just as it's hard to know the origin of magic, it's equally difficult to determine the origins of witchcraft. We have evidence from burial sites, cave paintings, and artifacts found across Europe and the Middle East that early humans relied on shamans to guide them in their hunts, keep knowledge about varieties of healing plants, and bring messages from the ancestors. This was usually done by transforming the shaman's spirit into an animal and then having that shaman-animal journey to other realms to find answers.

Prehistoric people weren't monotheists, and they weren't even really "pagan" yet—they were animists who believed the world was alive with spirits and that by talking to these spirits they could learn secrets about how the world worked. Shamans were people who spent their lives learning how to communicate and work with the spirit world on behalf of their communities and tribes.

Well after the Neolithic period, stories of witches started to emerge, like the Witch of Endor in the Bible, who acted as a necromancer to Saul to summon the prophet Samuel. We are also told in this passage that this was a last resort for Saul, who, as the first king of Israel, expelled all witches, magicians, and mediums from the land. It's interesting to see the beginning of a turn away from shamans and spirit workers to formalized priests associated with kings and rulers. It's probably around this time, if not earlier, that you see this division of magic start to happen.

This story can also tell us a couple of other things about what people thought about witches in the ancient Middle East. The first is that they weren't very well liked or trusted. The second is that people still used their services, even if they persecuted them publicly.

Then we have witches like the strix of ancient Rome, the lamia of Greece, and the lilitu in ancient Sumer. These witches are all variations on a myth about women who could turn into owls and steal away children—or even your soul—in the middle of the night. Stories of demonic women stealing babies and shape-shifting to cause mayhem would be standard fare for witches for thousands of years.

Right at the outset we have the witch as a person who works with spirits, like in the Bible, and the witch who is a spirit themselves, as told in folklore. One thing you'll see a lot as you study witchcraft is that there is a divide between the mythical, or "archetypal," witch and humans who practice witchcraft, but that divide is not always clear or wide.

CUNNING PEOPLE AND THE WITCH TRIALS

In the interest of time, I'm going to zip ahead a little bit.

The idea of what a witch is, from the conical hat to the black cat, comes largely from the medieval and early modern period in Europe, due in part to the witch trials of that time. Because of this, if you study witchcraft in depth, you'll be spending a lot of time in these eras.

Studying witchcraft is difficult, in part because for most of history "witch" wasn't something you called yourself; it was something you were called, usually with deadly consequences. The word *witch* wasn't really a good word, or a good thing to be called, until very recently in human history. And even today being called a witch will get you killed in many countries.

At this pivotal moment in the early modern period in Europe two "witches" emerged—the creature of folklore and the (usually) woman accused. The folkloric witches whom people feared, did magic against, and blamed for all sorts of ills were viewed as monsters, with very little separating them from the lamia or strix of old. For example, the Romanian word *strigoi* can translate to both "vampire" and "witch." (Much more *The Witch* than *Practical Magic.*)

On the other hand, you had the people we might look back on from today's perspective and call witches, but who themselves would have pushed this label away. In most villages and towns in Europe, and many parts of the world, there were people who knew charms and spells, held herbal knowledge, delivered babies, and worked magic on behalf of their neighbors. While there are many regional names for these people, we'll call them cunning folk for now.

There was a clear distinction made, at least by practitioners, between cunning craft and witchcraft. One of these was good and one was bad. These days, however, we look back at the folk healers and cunning folk of old as witches whose power was misunderstood—even though in all likelihood those very people would have flatly refused this term. Why?

For one, a lot of cunning folk were tried and killed as witches, either for their reputations or for the tools they used. Remember those grimoires from earlier, with all the demons and spells? Possession of a book like that could, and did, get people killed.

So are witches—at least medieval and early modern witches—purely a myth? Were there no covens or devil worshippers, but instead simply whispered tales of women in the woods that would steal away your soul? That's not quite true either. Again, the history of witchcraft is *complicated*.

Let's look at a hypothetical to demonstrate what I mean. Imagine if, hundreds of years from now, all the Marvel movies were deleted from history, but all the discussion, reviews, and fan fiction about them stuck around. It would be pretty hard to tell what, exactly, the movies were, and some people might believe they never existed at all. Witchcraft in early modern Europe is very similar. Reading through document after document of the witch trials, it's hard to believe *something* wasn't going on, even if that thing is difficult to imagine today. One woman who gives us a bit of insight into this, a peek behind the curtain of time, is a Scottish witch named Isobel Gowdie. This woman is significant in the history of witchcraft because in 1662 she confessed to being a witch. She wasn't coerced or forced through unimaginable torture to say whatever the hell would make the pain stop. Instead, she freely offered up her testimony and in so doing gives a more credible idea of what witchcraft might have actually looked like at the time.

We don't know much about Gowdie or her husband, and most records of them come from either her confessions or documents written about her after she died. She was probably in her thirties or forties when she confessed, and likely had no children. What we do know are the fantastical stories she told local authorities over the course of six weeks. Gowdie speaks of belonging to a coven that met in the wilderness. She tells of sending her spirit flying to a sabbath, not only with the devil in attendance, but the king and queen of fairy as well. It's this part about fairies that lends further credence to her testimony, as fairies weren't a Christian idea that had been imported to Scotland—they were a relic of an earlier, animist understanding of the land.

In addition to spirit flight, meetings with the devil, and spirits that worked for her, Gowdie describes several chants she used to shape-shift and work magic.

To change into a rabbit, she would chant:

> *I shall go into a hare,*
> *With sorrow, sych, and meickle care*
> *And I shall go in the Devil's name,*
> *Ay while I come home again*

And to change back she would chant:

> *Hare, hare, God send thee care.*
> *I am in a hare's likeness now,*
> *But I shall be in a woman's likeness even now.*

Here, once again, we have animal transformation and a reliance on both the devil and God as the sources of magic—a true crossroads that is not fully good, but not fully evil either.

I return to Isobel Gowdie often when I try to think of what witches of the past might have looked like, because she feels like a rare behind-the-scenes moment in history. It's not enough to form a full picture of witchcraft at the time, but it allows an outline, at least, to emerge.

A thread begins to appear here that we don't have time to follow in this book, but it's one I recommend following if you continue to study witchcraft and magic in general. Fittingly, witchcraft doesn't so much explain itself to us as leave a trail of breadcrumbs, letting us draw our own conclusions. Those accused of witchcraft were said to change shape into animal form, like Gowdie states above, and use animals like cats and dogs as *familiars*—aids in doing magical work. Doesn't this sound an awful lot like the shamans of old, who changed shape into animal form or had animal and spirit guides to help them?

Consider, too, that many accused witches were denounced because they possessed grimoires, which we now know contained spells and incantations that sometimes dated back to the ancient world. It does seem like something quite old is surviving here, maybe without practitioners themselves even realizing it. It might not have been the unified cult that some would later claim, but I do think it's interesting, to say the least, that when European colonists arrived in North America they compared the shamans and medicine people that Indigenous tribes had to their own cunning folk.

To recap, we now have both the mythical witch and the real people who worked *maleficium,* or magic for causing harm, and maybe were part of some small local cults.

Eventually, the world was forced to change in violent ways. Between the witch trials, the scientific revolution, and colonialism, magic was elbowed out of European life and witches became nothing more than myth, a shadow of an earlier, more brutal time that we've put behind us. For a long time, things were quiet.

But this all changed in the early twentieth century when a new, pagan form of witchcraft would be created.

WICCA AND THE MODERN WITCHCRAFT REVIVAL

For a while, modernity seemed to triumph over magic. Just like the grimoires, astrology, and sorcery of all kinds, magic became a silly, uncivilized thing of the past for about two hundred years. That is, until the latter half of the nineteenth century.

We've talked a lot in this book about the nineteenth century and the massive impact its occult revival had on the history of magic. This time period wasn't important for witchcraft itself, but it was critical for the groundwork it would lay for a future witchcraft revival. Because of something called the Witchcraft Act of

1542, it was *still* illegal to claim to have magical powers, or claim to be a witch, in the UK until 1951. Why this law didn't apply to books like *Psychic Self Defence* or *Magick in Theory and Practice* is a question I'll leave to legal scholars. Regardless, in the nineteenth century there were no public witchcraft covens or popular books published like there were for ceremonial magic, but this time period did provide a foundation for what was to come. Rituals, ideas, and symbols created or popularized by groups like the Golden Dawn and figures like Aleister Crowley would become the bedrock of modern Wicca and the witchcraft revival.

But, before we get to that, we have to talk about one of the most influential books of all time—which few people have ever heard of.

In 1921 an Egyptologist named **Margaret Murray** published a book called *The Witch-Cult in Western Europe*. While few people who aren't complete nerds know about this book today (this includes you now), one could argue that this was one of the most impactful books of the early twentieth century. Murray's theories changed how the public saw the history of witchcraft, which then changed how people saw witches and witchcraft. People still cite her theories today—not knowing where they came from—and she was so groundbreaking at the time that she even gets a shout-out in the opening lines of H. P. Lovecraft's most popular short story, *The Call of Cthulhu*. The only problem, as we'll see in a bit, is that she was completely wrong.

Murray theorized that witchcraft was the continuation of an ancient, pan-European pagan religion and the witch trials were the final attempt of the Church to get rid of this blasphemous rival. She believed witches worshipped a God and Goddess, namely the Roman goddess Diana and a figure known as "the Horned God," often represented by the gods Pan or Cernunnos. She postulated that this religion still existed, just in secret. While this is a great story, it is completely baseless. (Bummer, I know.) We have no evidence of a unified goddess religion that was stamped out by the Church; the people persecuted in the trials were almost all Christian; and a lot of evidence Murray cites has been warped to fit her theory.

As untrue as this idea is, it's likely you've heard of it. If you have, that's because it was hugely inspirational to a man named **Gerald Gardner**. Gardner was born to a wealthy English family in 1884. When he was young, he was sent to live in India, then a colony of the British Empire, for his health. While there, he became fascinated with Hinduism and the deep spiritual traditions of the subcontinent.

Upon returning to England in 1936, Gardner moved to the small town of Highcliffe, where he claimed to be initiated into a coven of witches in the nearby New Forest. There, he heard the word *wicca* used and learned the ways of witchcraft. Already very familiar with the writings of Margaret Murray and her witch-cult theory, he decided this must surely be one of those surviving witch cults, itself an offshoot of an ancient pagan cult. He later wrote about this experience in the book *Witchcraft Today* in 1954, and with it created the religion known as Wicca.

Let's pause for a second here, because there's a bit to unpack. A lot of people see Gardner as an unreliable narrator in this story, and even many Wiccans agree he probably exaggerated parts of his story. It's really up to you to decide how much you want to believe. Did he make the whole thing up? Did he really meet an ancient coven and copy down exactly what they told him?

For the record, here's what I think. I believe this happened and he really did go to a magical gathering of some sort, but I don't believe Gardner drew the correct conclusions from his encounter. We have evidence from the Museum of Witchcraft and Magic in Boscastle and other historical records that cunning craft was still being practiced in the UK at this time. I'm willing to give Gardner the benefit of the doubt and say that, sure, he met a group of people practicing full-on witchcraft. As we've already gone over though, witchcraft up until this point was not a religion—it was not the survival of a pagan cult nor formalized in the way it would be later. I think he basically took an idea from a group of people and ran with it, as if Tom Cruise had left the party in *Eyes Wide Shut* and made a religion out of it. You might think he made the whole thing up, or you might think he encountered something more serious than I am willing to believe. Draw your own conclusions.

What we do know for certain is that after this, Gardner set about creating and formalizing what he called Wicca, using this encounter as a base and adding in things from preexisting magical practices. In a way, everything you've learned in this book so far went into the creation of Wicca. The pentagram came from the grimoires; the ritual of drawing a circle came from the Golden Dawn and Crowley (remember the LBRP?); the grades of initiation and ritual were taken from the Masons; and the rest is a blend of Margaret Murray's ideas, grimoire magic, and metaphysical ideas picked up in India.

Now, it would be all too easy to dismiss Wicca because it is "made up." As a baby Wiccan in high school, I remember how disappointed and angry I was to learn that Wicca wasn't the oldest religion in the world and I wasn't practicing magic the same way witches throughout history had. Wicca tells a great, simple, and compelling story that you want to put yourself into. So learning that much of it was mashed together not even a hundred years ago can be frustrating. I personally have some issues with the Wiccan theology and worldview, and I've been to some circles (Wiccan gatherings) that felt less like ritual and more like dress-up.

However, I want you to remember that you are holding a book on *magic* in your hands, and it isn't a good look to hold a book like that and take yourself too seriously. The truth is, Wicca is one of the few religions we've seen form and spread in real time—a luxury we don't have with the major religions of the world. I will be the first to say that parts of Wicca are downright silly to me, but who's to say the twelve disciples weren't also wearing crushed-velvet robes?

So what is Wicca, what types of Wicca are there, and how is it different from other forms of witchcraft?

In general, Wiccans believe in a supreme God and Goddess and hold that all other gods and goddesses are permutations of those two main archetypes. Usually, the Goddess is more emphasized in Wicca than the God, and this god-

TRIPLE GODDESS

dess archetype is broken into three parts: the Maiden, the Mother, and the Crone, otherwise known as the Triple Goddess. The god archetype is often called "the Horned God" and associated with deities like Pan and Cernunnos.

Wiccans hold monthly rituals on the full moon and sabbaths on eight holy days of the year, known as the Wheel of the Year. Although these are often described as "ancient Celtic holidays," there's a lot of historical debate over those claims. Wiccans call themselves witches and practice magic, but most maintain you should only do benefic magic and shouldn't interfere with others' free will.

I want to talk for a moment about words we use to describe magic and how they have changed. For a long time—and sometimes to this day—people have described magic as *white* for good and *black* for bad. It's my and others' belief that there's a lot of negative racial implications going on here. Why is white good and black bad? Furthermore, it's confusing. Nowadays when I read "black magic," I think someone is referring to something like hoodoo or rootwork—you know, magic that Black people created—and it's not immediately clear that they mean "bad." Over the years, people have moved away from this language, but we've still encountered problems. Some will use *high* or *low* magic (which we've already discussed the problems of) and others will say *left-* and *right*-hand magic, to mean "bad" or "good" respectively. Beyond class implications and misinterpretations of Buddhist philosophy going on here, there's still a lack of moral clarity. Is magic done to harm others bad if it's in self-defense? Is magic done for material gain of "lower" value?

Personally, I think we should move to using *malefic* to mean magic done to harm or cause pain, and *benefic* to mean magic done for positive or generative purposes. First off, they sound cooler, and second, they encompass a greater complexity within magic. Okay, rant over.

This is in accordance with the main moral code of Wicca, which comes from the final line of the *Wiccan Rede*: "an ye harm none, do what ye will." (It's not hard to see the Crowley influence from "do what thou wilt.") Traditionally, you had to be initiated into Wicca by other Wiccans, and in some covens you still must, but today many members "self-initiate" into Wicca. The symbol of Wicca is the pentagram.

THE PENTAGRAM

The *pentacle* is a five-pointed star within a circle. It is commonly used as the religious symbol for Wicca and sometimes for witchcraft in general. It's different from a *pentagram*, which is just a boring star with no circle.

The history of the pentagram goes back a long way (it turns out people have always loved drawing stars), but its association with witchcraft is somewhat recent.

Before bad boy Aleister Crowley came along to shake up the occult world in the late nineteenth century, there was another magician who completely redefined the world of magic. In fact, he's the one who coined the term *occult*.

Eliphas Levi was a French magician and revolutionary who essentially brought magic into the modern world. Pentacles had been used a lot in the grimoires, but it was Levi who made them an occult symbol on their own. Drawing on ideas from the Middle Ages, Levi said the pentagram, a pentacle surrounded by a circle, was a symbol for the universe itself, with the star being the human body both created and surrounded by the universe. He aligned the pentagram with the four elements—the fifth point representing the spirit—and said it could be used for protection and banishing, not just spirit summoning. In the same way you don't usually hear people blasting Beethoven out of their cars, Levi isn't really talked about much in popular occultism today. However, the pentagram is perhaps the best example of just how far his reach has extended.

Gerald Gardner, as a student of the grimoires and Levi's work, wrote about the pentagram a lot in his personal diaries, and because of this, it was made the official symbol of Wicca as the religion gained popularity.

PENTACLE

After Gardner's death in 1964, Wicca continued to spread. Gardner's student—and my favorite early Wiccan—Dorene Valiente wrote "The Charge of the Goddess," a speech now recited at most Wiccan ceremonies. She also went on to champion the idea of self-initiation, rather than initiation by other Wiccans.

This is a bit of a side quest, but I throw it out in case you, like me, are interested in weird witchcraft. Other witches came out of the woodwork after the Witchcraft Laws were repealed, and while Gardner was the most impactful and famous among them, he wasn't the only one. Witches like **Robert Cochrane** would form the basis of what we now call traditional witchcraft, with orders like the Clan of Tubal Cain. **Traditional witchcraft** is a form of witchcraft that places emphasis on folklore and folk traditions surrounding European witchcraft. It's usually regional in nature and emphasizes personalizing your craft to suit the land you are practicing on. Pre- to early Wiccan rituals act as a grounding influence across practitioners. Ritual items usually include a stang, a broom, a chalice, and a dagger.

Cochrane claimed he was initiated into witchcraft through his family, but, in a similar way, I once claimed to be Elliot Page at a nightclub. What I'm trying to say is that this claim is dubious. Valiente didn't buy it, and I trust her opinion on this matter. However, Cochrane was a great witch and inspired people at the time and for generations to come. He started a modern witchcraft that was grounded in historical roots but evolved based on the times, and for that I'm personally grateful. If things like cunning craft and really old-school witchcraft pique your interest, consider reading more about traditional witchcraft.

Okay, side quest over, let's get back to the main story.

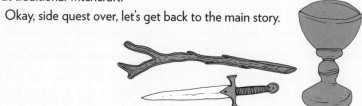

In the 1960s, Gardner's student Raymond Buckland brought Wicca to the United States, where it found a welcome home in the '60s counterculture. It's in this cauldron that modern ideas about Wicca and witchcraft as feminist, free-spirit spirituality come about.

In 1979, a very important book in the history of witchcraft was published. *The Spiral Dance* by Starhawk would go on to be a best seller for years to come and would form the foundation of many modern ideas of witchcraft as an inherently political, feminist religion.

While I think this is a valid interpretation of modern witchcraft, these ideas are all very recent additions to witchcraft. Starhawk admits in the introduction to the twentieth anniversary edition of the *Spiral Dance* that she knew nothing about witchcraft or covens when she started teaching it and only discovered Wicca after already having taught a course on witchcraft and female spirituality.

In response to criticisms of the misleading or outright false histories she gives throughout the book, Starhawk claims she was writing a "mythic history" and can't be held to a high standard when it comes to historical accuracy—after all, she wasn't writing a PhD thesis. I would argue that it's more important to be as accurate as possible in a book being published by a major publisher and read by millions than in a thesis that will most likely only be read by a dozen or so at most (sorry, grad students), but what do I know?

I want to pause for a moment to dig into a few things around gender and identity that regularly come up around witchcraft. While I think it's important to keep in mind the historical context for the persecution discussed earlier, I'm not downplaying the role that sexism had in the witch trials or accusations of witchcraft. They obviously did since, while people of all genders were tried for witchcraft, it was mostly women and feminine people who were targeted and killed. On top of that, the degrading physical examinations and torture accused witches would undergo once arrested point clearly to some serious sexual exploitation. The witch trials weren't really seen through a political lens, let alone a feminist one, until the 1960s and '70s, and that fact doesn't take away from the validity of this interpretation. Still, it is important to understand witchcraft wasn't seen as feminist until very recently in human history. Consider also that Gardner himself was a conservative Tory who saw Wicca as a potentially nationalist religion for Britain, and the argument for a clean equation that witchcraft equals feminism begins to get murky. Because of its history, I think it's reasonable to adopt the term *witch* as a feminist moniker. But I also think it's good to keep in mind that what we are doing is reclaiming a negative, pejorative word, rather than taking on one that was once positive.

There's another myth here that's worth pushing back on, as well. People were not persecuted for witchcraft because they were witches. I know that's hard to wrap your head around at first, but think of it as similar to the way certain groups are viewed or targeted as criminals in contemporary society. Now, let's relate that back to our question of witches in early modern Europe. If you practiced magic, particularly malefic types of magic, were you a witch? Well, that depends on how much money you had, how many people liked you, and what your status in society was. (With that in mind, I will emphasize, as I have before, that if you call yourself a witch in the twenty-first century, it is your job to understand these networks of power and how criminality is politically determined, and then work to undo them.) Being a "witch" was, in many ways, a legal term imposed upon people who often weren't practicing witchcraft or considered themselves witches in order to consolidate the newly emerging state's power.

So back to Starhawk. I don't want to bash her or the people she inspired. I'm one of those people, after all, and as someone who also wrote a book about witchcraft and politics, I have to applaud her for being the person who combined the two and acknowledge that I traverse a path she paved for me. (I also have to applaud her for pushing back on some of the transphobic and gender essentialist corners of Wicca before those issues were being widely discussed.) However, for the sake of historical accuracy, and in the interest of preserving the actual histories of the women who were persecuted for the crime of witchcraft, we have to correct the record. Feminism and witchcraft can absolutely go hand in hand, and I think to do that we have to believe that both can stand firmly on the grounds of actual history, not fantasy.

As of this writing, Wicca has fallen quite a bit in popularity, but for a while it was pretty much the only game in town if you wanted to study magic—maybe Thelema or chaos magic if you were lucky. I was a Wiccan for a few years, partially because it spoke to me and partially because I didn't know there were other paths available.

With all the occult content now online it might be hard to imagine a time when one perspective so dominated the conversation. Today people often want to stand out by expressing a unique take on witchcraft or magic, but back in the day—approximately 1980–2010—in order to practice magic you had to interact with Wicca on some level. I really want to emphasize this: Wicca was so huge that *Buffy the Vampire Slayer, Sex and the City, Charmed,* and many more movies and shows in the late twentieth century referenced it. In the 2000s Wicca was the fastest-growing religion in the United States, with adherents in the tens of thousands. Wiccans fought legal civil rights battles, the consequences of which reverberate to this day, and Wicca was used as "evidence" to send three wrong-fully accused teenagers to jail in the infamous West Memphis Three trial. With all this history, it is honestly shocking to me how quickly Wicca seems to have faded from public consciousness in the past decade. You might not be a Wiccan—and might even roll your eyes at it—but you need to understand Wicca and its impact on witchcraft to be a good student of magic.

It's important to know all this because Wicca basically claimed all of witchcraft for several decades. As someone who has done many interviews over the years on witchcraft, I can tell you that the record I usually have to set straight isn't that witches are green or eat babies, it's the idea that witch-craft is a religion, this religion was persecuted during the witch trials, and there's nothing malefic in its history or practice at all. These are all ideas that come directly from Wicca, and we are only just starting to get out from under them now.

WITCHCRAFT TODAY

Wicca continued to rise in prominence for decades, essentially becoming the face of modern witchcraft by the end of the twentieth century. This isn't an issue in and of itself—Wicca is a fulfilling religion to many—but there were several lies that Wicca promoted, particularly post-*The Spiral Dance*, that have come under a lot of scrutiny in the past few years. A non-exhaustive list is:

- ◆ Witchcraft is and has always been a religion.
- ◆ Witchcraft is inherently pagan.
- ◆ Wicca is the oldest religion in the world.
- ◆ Wiccans were persecuted and subjected to genocide during "The Burning Times."
- ◆ Witchcraft has nothing to do with the devil.
- ◆ Witches don't harm people with magic.

I hope by now you can see how silly and, quite frankly, offensive these statements are. Yet they were pushed so hard, for so long, by so many Wiccan authors that many of these misstatements became mainstream talking points.

In 1999 Professor Ronald Hutton published a book that, over time, shifted the foundation under Wicca. *Triumph of the Moon* is probably the most comprehensive book on modern pagan witchcraft ever written. It didn't attack Wicca, and Hutton seems to have a great deal of affection for Wiccans, witches, and modern pagans, but his book debunked most of the historical claims made by Wiccans.

This was a mountain of research Wicca just couldn't come back from, and I think it's fair to say we are now in a post-Hutton world when it comes to modern witchcraft. There are still lies, there are still bogus claims, and the grifters will always be with you, but the zeal that once accompanied Wicca has diminished somewhat.

We could go right into what witchcraft means today. We could dive into all the delicious *discourse* on the subject, but I think it's more important to reflect on all we just talked about.

It's hard sometimes to pull out a consistent thread in the history of witch-craft, but if I had to choose one, it's a longing to find an eternal, unbroken magical current that connects us back to an ancient lineage.

I sometimes joke that Wicca was the first person to break my heart. I remember when I found it, I thought I had come to something special, ancient, and unchanging. When I learned that Wicca was essentially made up a few decades ago and that there was no old-time goddess cult that had survived to the present day, which I was lucky enough to discover, I was devastated. Was what I was doing even real? Was it even possible to be a witch?

Sometimes I think people run from history, especially the history of magic, because they are afraid of explaining all the wonder and magic away. I think this is especially true when it comes to young women and the history of witchcraft, because the story Wicca tells feels *emotionally* true. The idea of a once powerful, female-centered religion that was destroyed by a patriarchal church and forced underground, where it became the twisted specter of a witch, describes through myth the process of socialization most girls undergo in Western society. At some point, you are told that who and what you are at your core are bad or need correcting somehow. The essential power you had before society told you about this brokenness gets taken or deformed into something angry and bitter. While this is obviously not true for everyone who is drawn to Wicca, I think it is one reason why this myth refuses to die.

I'm a big believer that it's best not to base your understanding of history on vibes. This is equally true for ugly things like slavery and war and beauti-ful things like spirituality and magic. It might be disappointing to hear that there really is no unified witchcraft, no surviving pagan religion, and no single through line that unites all these things. I would urge you, however, not to run from this truth and not to let it make you bitter.

Let's imagine for a moment that your family is of Italian origin. Your grandma has a "famous" red-sauce recipe that she claims has been handed down through generations, through your whole family line, going back for thousands of years. The thing is, this is impossible. Tomatoes were only introduced to Italy in the fifteenth or sixteenth century. Knowing this, do you call your sweet Nona a liar and denounce her recipe as an inauthentic forgery? Or do you recognize that history is, by definition, a record of how things change in a culture? That even if this recipe only goes back a couple generations, it is by this time traditional because you keep choosing to use it?

In my opinion, there are actually four "witchcrafts": the ancient and "shamanic," the cunning craft, the goddess-centered pagan religion, and the chaos magic–inspired blend that is popular today. Rather than abandoning witchcraft entirely because of these differences, saying a true witchcraft never existed at all, or shouting "*WELL, ACTUALLY*" over each other online, I would submit to you that these different tracks are *all* valid forms of witchcraft, so long as we acknowledge the others.

Now that you know these different forms of witchcraft and their histories, I leave it up to you to discover which one calls to you, if any, and to further your studies there.

JOURNAL PROMPTS

◆ What does the word *witch* mean to me? What feelings, images, and emotions come up for me when I call myself that word?

◆ Does the word *witch* "fit" me, or does it not feel quite right? If I had to come up with a name for my magical practice, what would it be?

◆ Which of the four witchcrafts in this chapter resonates with me the most? Is it a combination of several?

◆ Who are the witches today? Who is treated in our society now the way accused witches were in the past?

◆ Would I like to practice magic with a coven or by myself?

ACTIVITY

FULL MOON SCRYING

There are technically a lot of activities and rituals I could put here. Witchcraft is a magical art that picks up things from all over and runs with them. However, I've already given you a way to cast a circle and protect yourself with the LBRP, a way to make familiars with the servitor, and a candle magic working. With a little outer practice starting to form, I think it's time to turn the eye inward and focus on scrying.

Scrying is a form of divination that involves looking into a shiny or dark surface long enough that you begin to see images and shapes. We've all seen the iconic image of a witch looking into their crystal ball with a client shifting nervously in a seat across from them, but crystals aren't the only way to do this.

Scrying can be used to divine the future, but it can also be used as a substitute for meditation and journeying and as a way to speak to spirits, the dead, and our ancestors. It's a very far-reaching magical skill, and one worth giving a try.

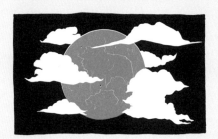

For this, you will need:

A dark bowl, cup, or some sort of vessel for water

A full moon

A black candle

A quiet room or closet where you can be alone

On the night of a full moon, take a bowl of water out to a quiet place. If you can be alone outside, do so and sit under the moon. Make sure you can see the full moon reflected in the still surface of the water. If you can't go outside for this, go to a dark room, turn off all the lights, and light your candle. Again, make sure the light from the candle is reflected in the water.

Take a moment to breathe deeply and think of whom you would like to speak to or what you would like to scry on. Remember, pretty much anything is on the table here.

When you have a clear idea in your mind, speak your request into the water. It doesn't have to be elaborate. Simply saying "I would like to talk with my grandmother" or "Show me what danger lies ahead of me" will work fine.

Gaze into the water and let your vision start to swirl and go blurry. I like to stare just to the left of the light source reflected in the water, but many like to stare directly at it.

Eventually, you will see shapes, colors, faces, or even whole scenes play out in front of you. Usually, the longer you sit, the more vivid your visions will become.

Only you can know when the time to end your scrying will be. It might be when you get your answer, when your head starts to hurt, or just when you get spooked. When you are done, thank the spirits that have joined you, and end the ritual. You might want to leave an offering of bread or water, but that isn't necessary.

I recommend cleansing and grounding after scrying, since it can be an intense experience for many. After you have done this, write down what you saw in your magic journal.

FURTHER READING

Traditional Witchcraft: A Cornish Book of Ways, **Gemma Gary**
A great introduction to practicing witchcraft, grounded in history and local lore. Spells, oil formulas, rituals, holidays, and tools are all outlined here in a direct and simple manner. All of Gary's books are great, but if you want to have a formal witchcraft practice, without relying on Wicca, check this book out.

Triumph of the Moon: A History of Modern Pagan Witchcraft, **Ronald Hutton**
I mentioned this book within the chapter, but it's worth bringing up again. It's not only a great history of modern witchcraft, but of Western occultism in general. A very dense but fascinating read, check this book out if you want to go well beyond any of the history I talk about in this book.

Witchcraft Medicine: Healing Arts, Shamanic Practices, and Forbidden Plants,
Claudia Müller-Ebeling, Christian Rätsch, Wolf-Dieter Storl, PhD
If plants, herbal medicine, and folklore appeal to you, this book is a wealth of knowledge. It traces the history of plants often associated with witches and looks back at the ways ancient peoples used them, the goddesses they were associated with, and the scientific properties of said plants.

PAGANISM, GODS, AND HISTORY

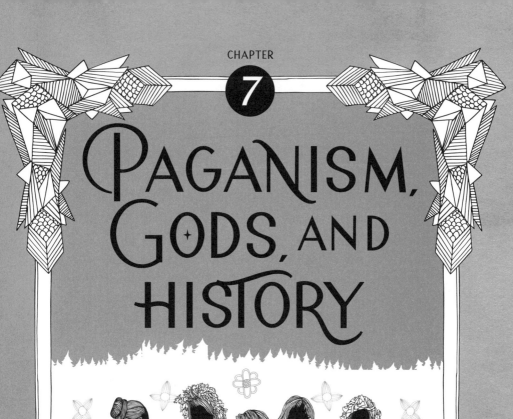

We're going to round out *How to Study Magic* with what is perhaps the least explicitly "magical" chapter. If magic is about changing your reality, making things happen in physical reality, or, as Crowley famously said, "the art and science of causing change in accordance with the Will," then paganism seems a little different. Sure, many pagan deities get used in magic, but if you're taking a chaos magic approach, you might only see these gods as a useful means to an end or psychological ideas we can ritually dramatize.

Paganism, on the other hand, might not be about making things happen or gaining practical results. It might be a more spiritual or religious way of contextualizing and understanding the world.

Like Wicca, paganism has gone through surges and dips in popularity, and people's relationship to it has changed a lot in the last few years.

Today it seems like being a pagan and practicing magic are synonymous. Every book you pick up, video you watch, or blog you read seems to talk about ancient gods and pre-Christian religions. It's true that most magical people these days aren't Christian in the strict sense of the word, and most do work with pre-Christian gods in their practices. However, as we've seen throughout this book, plenty of Christians, Jews, and Muslims have practiced magic throughout the years without considering themselves pagan. If you come from an Abrahamic background and you don't want to give that up, remember you don't actually have to.

However, if you feel called to worship pre-Christian gods, want to recreate an ancestral spiritual practice, or simply want to work with mythic figures in your existing magical practice, then you should get acquainted with paganism.

In this chapter, I'm going to go over a bit of the history of modern paganism, introduce you to different types of paganism, and give you some tips and tricks for getting started.

Since this topic is very broad—globe-spanning, even—I won't be able to go into every god, goddess, pantheon, or philosophy out there. Additionally, there are a ton of ways to go about being a pagan, mostly because people stopped doing that for about a thousand years and we're picking up where they left off after a long game of telephone. Because of that, I'm going to be speaking from a lot of personal experience to make things somewhat simpler. Keep that in mind if something I say doesn't work or resonate with you, and as always, keep exploring after you put this book down.

HISTORY

The term *pagan* comes from the Latin *paganus,* which means "tied to the land." This might sound very romantic today, but in ancient Rome it was a derisive term city dwellers used for farmers and peasants. It was basically the ancient equivalent of calling someone a redneck.

Think about that for a second. When we call ourselves pagan today, we are thinking of something totally different than ancient people would have. Today, *paganism* is a term that tries to unify a broad coalition of people who practice aspects of pre-Christian religion, but back in the day it was an insult. Imagine jumping two thousand years in the future to a time when Christianity has been long extinct, but there are people trying to revive it. Everything from Catholicism to Pentecostal snake-handling has been collapsed under one big umbrella of "Redneckism," in which people try to worship the way ancient Christians did. This is basically what a lot of neopaganism is, or has been, over the last few decades. What I'm saying is, we should be humble about just how much we can know about ancient spirituality.

I'm sure you know that as Christianity spread, the pre-Christian religions and traditional folkloric beliefs of Europe died off. What's important to remember is that this wasn't a clean, organized, or uniform process. Some countries, like Lithuania, weren't Christianized until the 1300s, while others, like Iceland, pretty much converted in name only. Some people were only converted after prolonged violence and oppression, while others went fairly peacefully. In pretty much all cases, pre-Christian beliefs, spirits, holy spaces, and even gods simply didn't go away and survived through Catholic saints and

folk magic, an excellent place to start your research if you are interested in paganism.

Beginning in the nineteenth century (of course) people in Europe, particularly aristocrats and the wealthy, became interested in the ancient religions of their homelands. Some of this was silly fun for rich people; some came from a romantic impulse to live as the ancients did; and some would later take on a sinister edge. It's important to keep in mind that the modern nation-state is a fairly recent concept that really came into its own during this period. Part of getting people on board with this concept was making the case that a certain group of people had always, and would always, be in a certain spot on earth. From there, it was important to create the narrative of an unbroken ethnic line going back to the ancient world. It's why the Grimm Brothers began collecting German folklore, why Richard Wagner wrote operas about Northern European myths, and why the English aristocracy sometimes dressed up like druids. It's also why, later on, groups like the Nazis would try to revive the swastika as an ancient Germanic symbol for the sun and why Benito Mussolini's fascist party would adopt the Roman symbol of the axe and sticks tied together.

Right here, we have our first lesson about paganism, and one we'll spend more time examining later. History isn't neutral, and people are always trying to tell a certain story about the past to justify political action in the present. There are lots of people, from the recent past up to today, who want there to be a clear ethnic or cultural line that extends from the ancient world and will justify why they have the right to live somewhere and other people don't. I want you to be skeptical when you hear people talk this way, because you will, since the evidence we have indicates that people in the past didn't see spirituality this way. Ancient Scandinavians traded with and were friendly to Muslims; Romans, Egyptians, and Greeks swapped gods all the time; and the lines between where one god's worship started and another's began were often very blurry. That doesn't mean we can't see distinct differences where we find them or that we should give up on recreating old practices and ideas at all, but fascism, nationalism, and xenophobia are popular in part because they are simple answers to a complex world; I want you to embrace complexity as you study paganism.

Anyway, while paganism of a sort experienced short-lived popularity because of romanticism and nationalism, it wasn't until the 1950s and '60s that it became the hippie-influenced thing we know today.

We talked about this in the last chapter, but just to review in this context: paganism really came to the United States through Wicca in the 1960s. At the time, the country was in the midst of incredible political change and ideas about feminism, environmentalism, and free love were becoming more and more popular.

Embracing these ideas caused many to move away from traditional, monotheistic religions. At the same time, they still had spiritual needs to meet and began looking for that fulfillment elsewhere. Many Americans were attracted to Asian religions like Hinduism or Buddhism, but others became interested in paganism, seeing it as a chance to create an earth-centered, female-empowered spiritual path.

It's around this time that the idea of paganism as a "worship of the earth" kind of religion really came into being. It makes sense in many ways, as plenty of old gods were said to dwell in rivers, mountains, and trees, but just like the political ideas that got put onto witchcraft and Wicca at this time, it's worth noting that, while valid, these are somewhat modern notions.

While Wicca laid the groundwork for a lot of modern paganism, other groups and orders soon followed, beginning in the 1960s and continuing through the 1990s. Around this time academics also started using the term *neopaganism* to describe modern pagans. It's totally fine if you want to use this label, but I think it sounds kind of '90s and tacky so I don't. To each their own.

While Wicca continues to dominate as the biggest branch of paganism, it's by no means the only game in town. Let's take a look at different forms of paganism and see what sets them apart.

TYPES OF MODERN PAGANISM

RECONSTRUCTIONIST VS. NON-RECONSTRUCTIONIST

While there are many forms of paganism, there are two major strains that most people fall on one side or the other of.

Reconstructionist pagans try to reconstruct the rituals, holidays, and beliefs of pre-Christian people as closely as possible.

Non-reconstructionist pagans take inspiration, gods, and lore from ancient people, but ultimately do their own thing.

For example, a modern Heathen might try to reconstruct pre-Christian Scandinavian belief systems, while a Wiccan might also worship Odin, but in a structure that these ancient people would not recognize.

I used to call myself a "reconstructionist Kemetic pagan," which translates to "other" on census forms. What I meant was that I tried to recreate and follow the religion of ancient Egypt as best I could. My morality was informed by this; the way I defined divinity came from this; and ultimately my worldview was contained in this. Eventually, I discovered that I'm polyamorous when it comes to divinity and can't pick just one pantheon to work with. Still, I sometimes look back wistfully on those days. There's something very nice and contained about being a reconstructionist. You may not cast your net wide, but you can cast it very deeply, and honestly, having a defined set of codes and rules can be very comforting.

Here's a short list of reconstructionist pagan religions and their symbols. Typically, these religions are based around certain **pantheons,** or groups of gods from a specific mythology.

CELTIC PAGANISM:
This symbol is called the triskele and was found on a Neolithic tomb in Ireland.

DRUIDRY:
Related to Celtic paganism, but druids tend to be a part of orders with degrees of initiation and skills one must learn.

HELLENISM:
Paganism relating to Greek and sometimes Roman pantheons.

HEATHENRY, ÁSATRU, AND ODINISM:
Let's just get this out of the way now: I've listed these names in the order of what is least to most likely to bring up a bunch of racist websites when you google it. We'll get into that more later. For now, these are all names of neopagan religions that are tied to Scandinavian and Norse pantheons.

KEMETIC PAGANISM:
Represented by the ankh, this relates to the religion of ancient Egypt, the original name of which was Kemet or "the black land," hence the word *Kemetic*.

There's something I want you to keep in mind about reconstructionist paganism, if it's something you choose to pursue. What we think of as the "official" mythology of an ancient culture is a somewhat modern, post-monotheist idea in itself.

In less fancy language, if you take a place like Egypt as an example, many of the gods that we think of as part of the overall, unified pantheon were once local gods who didn't have much to do with those in other areas of the Nile.

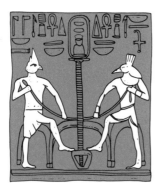

Horus, for instance, is looked at now as simply the king of the Egyptian pantheon, but scholars believe this only happened after the pharaoh of Upper Egypt, whose people originally worshipped Horus, expanded his rule into Lower Egypt and supplanted the main god there, who was Set. A similar thing happened to the Greek gods, who began as separate local deities, but were made into one big, incestuous family so that city-states in Greece could consolidate power. In places like Scandinavia and Northern Europe, the idea of a pantheon of gods or gods "of" something becomes even more foreign. A lot of our ideas about what ancient people even thought of as gods come from bad scholarship in the nineteenth century, and while some incredible research has been done in more recent years, these old ideas are hard to shake.

Another thing to keep in mind is that, as of the writing of this book, time travel hasn't been invented yet. This means that we can never actually know what people of the past did or thought daily. We have some good ideas and some strong guesses, but it's best to allow this distance to humble you, not discourage you.

At this point, I imagine you might be a little confused, or at least unsure of where to go next. Is paganism about earth worship, or isn't it? Do I have to pick one pantheon to work with, or can I choose several? If we don't know exactly what ancient people believed, did, or thought, then what are we supposed to do?

I think the best approach to questions like these is almost always to start small and simple and to go back to what you want to get out of your spirituality.

With that in mind, I think the easiest, and most typical, way to start practicing paganism is to pick a deity you want to work with and go from there.

DEVOTIONAL AND
TRANSACTIONAL RELATIONSHIPS

One thing you'll notice in books, blogs, and videos on paganism is that people typically say they "work with" a particular deity, rather than "worship" them. I like pointing this out because I've always found it a bit funny, as if Anubis were your coworker or something.

The other reason I think this wording is important to point out is because it reveals something about the nature of how people typically interact with deities and spirits in modern paganism. While devotional relationships exist, in which people worship a particular god or goddess just for the sake of it, most people typically expect to directly benefit from a relationship with gods down the line, even if it's just general help with their magic.

There are two broad ways you can break down working with deities: **devotional relationships** and **transactional relationships**. In a devotional relationship, you typically dedicate a day, time, or altar to a specific deity in order to maintain a more personal relationship with them. In a transactional relationship, you might just need to talk to Venus for a particular spell you are doing, and so you only make offerings or perform a certain ritual as a good gesture. These lines are often blurry, and throughout your practice you're likely to have both at different times, but I think it's good to remember that not every single interaction you have with a god has to be dramatic or long-term. Sometimes you just need to borrow a spiritual cup of sugar.

CHOOSING AND BEING CHOSEN

So how do you choose a deity to work with? Well, it depends!

First, take a minute to think about what you want to get out of a spiritual relationship with a deity. Perhaps you want help dealing with anger in a healthy way, so you want to strike up a relationship with Mars. Maybe you want to connect with your ancestors or deal with grief, so you work with Anubis. Maybe you've just always really liked a certain deity and want to see what a relationship with them would be like. And there are also those transactional relationships, in which you work only temporarily with a certain deity.

You can absolutely choose a deity, pantheon, or religion, and see how it fits. On the other hand, it's possible to be chosen by a deity, and in fact, I think this happens more than we think.

What do I mean when I say "chosen"? It sounds so dramatic, like you are The Chosen One™ or like this god has descended from the clouds and singled you out specifically for a special reason. Not to disappoint you, but that's not what I'm talking about, and if someone starts talking like that to you, I would politely walk away before they try to sell you essential oils.

Instead, this is more like someone approaching you at a party and striking up a conversation with the hope of being your friend. A deity or spirit might poke at you, spiritually speaking, in the hopes of working with you.

So what does this poking look like? Remember in chapter 2 when we talked about synchronicity? In my experience, synchronicity and dreams are the main ways deities will communicate with you when they are trying to get your attention.

If a certain deity is trying to get a hold of you, it should feel pretty obvious. The deity, and symbols associated with them, should be popping up in your dreams, in graffiti on the sidewalk, in random conversation, and in whatever media you happen to be consuming. Remember: if it feels like you have to force a connection between things you are experiencing throughout the day, it's not a synchronicity.

I'll give an example from my own life. Once I had an ancestor come through for me in a dream. I woke up and thought, "well, that was nice," but didn't ascribe much to it. Later that day, a podcast I was listening to mentioned something specific from this dream, then later that same word popped up in a show I was watching, then after that it came up again at work. When all of this became impossible to ignore, I left an offering to this ancestor and asked them to appear in another dream to confirm it was really them and I wasn't imagining it—and they did.

I want to say here that just because you get this invitation from a spirit or deity doesn't mean you have to accept it. I've found that once you really get into magic and are doing it pretty consistently, this kind of thing will happen from time to time. I've had plenty of deities leave me a trail of synchronicities to follow that I simply refused to or only followed to a point. At the risk of sounding like an Instagram infographic, boundaries are important—and this is just as true with spiritual beings as it is with material beings.

However, all this can be very exciting, and a little scary. It's in moments like this that you will remember that magic is *real* and the world is much weirder than we all think it is.

While there's no one way to confirm or continue a conversation with a spirit or deity once contact has been made, here's a simple formula that's worked for me and might be a good start for you.

① Synchronicity storm! You've had some weird things happen that all seem to be tied together, and you think they're worth pursuing.

② Divine on it. Break out your favorite divination method to get a read on the situation, and maybe even ask a friend if you don't feel you can be objective. Does the reading make you feel like this is "real" or a good thing to follow up on?

③ Assuming the answer is yes, ask for further communication. Leave a simple offering out overnight (bread, booze, water, or flowers work well) and ask whoever is talking to you to visit you in a dream and accept your offering as payment and thanks.

④ If they appear again, take some time to reflect on the messages that are coming through and the feelings you get. If this seems exciting or meaningful, feel free to follow that thread. If the messages stop, you can still do research and try to pursue a relationship, or just accept that a cool thing happened and you don't have to follow it further.

Think back to an idea we discussed in the grimoire chapter. Part of the reason why keeping a journal, magical or not, is important is because it lets you check in with your feelings, to see if your life is getting better or worse as a result of magic.

Devotion isn't always fun and sometimes involves doing things you don't really feel like doing as an act of devotion, but it should always leave you feeling better overall and lead you to positive places. Think of it like working out: There will be days you don't want to lift weights, go for a run, or even stretch, but you push yourself to do so because you know it will make you feel better. However, if you keep getting injuries while working out, keep pushing yourself well past your limits, or you and your life don't improve, but in fact get worse, then you should stop and figure out what's wrong.

Devotion can be work, but it shouldn't feel like a chore. If your mental health, personal relationships, financial situation, and/or life in general are suffering because of your spiritual practice, then you need to stop and reassess the situation. Go review myths from all over the world, as context can be really illuminating. Sometimes the gods want more from mortals than we can give, and when that happens, you have to remember that you are a person with free will and autonomy who can say no to certain relationships or requests, no matter who they come from.

UNVERIFIED PERSONAL GNOSIS

Inevitably, as you deepen your relationship with a particular deity, saint, spirit, or pantheon, you'll get certain vibes about things that they like, don't like, or are associated with. You'll check to see if there's any record or lore around this vibe. If you can't find any documentation, but the vibe keeps checking out for you, go with it. What you've just experienced is called *unverified personal gnosis*, or UPG for short.

UPG usually comes the longer and deeper your spiritual practice goes, and it can be a great sign that the relationship you are forming is dynamic and growing. An example of a UPG might be that you find the goddess Hekate really likes being offered apples. There's no real lore around this, but she seems to like it when you leave them for her.

When in doubt about how to start working with a particular deity, I always think the safest bet is to follow mythology, lore, and history for guidance, but once you get up and running, you should allow for UPG to come through and not push it away because it's not "official." There's no real danger in UPG, unless you rely solely on that and don't hear any outside input or try to push your own UPG on others as official doctrine. Remember, it's *personal* gnosis, and it's okay to have quirks in our own practices.

A NOTE ON RACISM AND APPROPRIATION

Before we leave this subject, I think we need to address some issues that have plagued modern paganism from the beginning. This conversation is going to get thorny and uncomfortable, but I think it's my job as someone who has been around the proverbial block a few times to talk about this with the newbies out there before you fall down some dark rabbit holes.

Let's start by identifying something called a *closed practice*. Confusion often accompanies this term, but put simply it means a religion or spiritual tradition that you must be initiated into in order to practice. This term usually refers to Indigenous or African Diasporic Religions, where very intense and strict initiation practices accompany entry into the religion. I'm talking about things like giving up wearing certain colors or eating certain foods, potentially for the rest of your life. This line is spiritual, not racial, and while technically anyone can be initiated into a closed practice if they are invited in, if you are a white person interested in practicing these specific traditions, it's imperative that you talk to and learn from people within these practices and go through the proper channels for initiation. The reason others, and myself, emphasize this around the spiritual practices of BIPOC people is because these very practices have been misunderstood, demonized, outlawed, and profited off of by people who aren't part of these traditions.

Now, on the other end, there has been an increasingly loud group of white people who use this same language of appropriation to keep people of color from practicing European paganism and who are engaged with "identity politics for white people." This is where we really must stand firm against violence and nonsense.

When you say that European paganism is closed and only white people can worship Norse gods, for instance, and try to hide that racism behind language about ancestry, you are either being so willfully ignorant that your literacy needs to be brought into question or you know exactly what you are doing and are acting maliciously. I'm a white person, and I know for a fact I would never be turned away from an Odinist gathering based on my ancestry. This is despite the fact that my ancestors aren't from Scandinavia, likely never worshipped those gods, and were in fact attacked, raped, and pillaged by Vikings. I know this because I have interviewed and spoken with more than a few Odinists and white supremacists.

You only have to look at the past few decades of European history to see that people on that continent don't always get along. In fact, I think it's safe to argue they mostly don't, with peace in that part of the world a bit of a historical anomaly. Whether or not someone is "really" French, German, English, or whatnot has been the cause of ethnic cleansing, repression, war, and conflict for centuries. Hell, to this day there are xenophobic English people who don't really see Polish people as "white." *White* is a construct, a made-up idea that came primarily from the United States as a way to bring together disparate peoples from Europe—who still held firm to their ethnic differences—to stand united against Black people and the threat of a Black uprising during and after slavery. If someone claims that a form of European paganism is for white people only, they are at best laughably ignorant about their own history and at worst a white supremacist. If you come across this—and you will—walk the other way and tell others to stay away as well.

At the end of the day, here's the thing about modern paganism. These are all new religions, even if they worship old gods and pull from historical records. Christianity and Islam became dominant thousands of years ago, while the original pagan religions trailed off and disappeared. No one has practiced them in a very long time. None of these are continuous practices followed by a persecuted minority, and as such, you can't really "appropriate" any of them. You can be disrespectful or stupid, but you can't really steal from a dead culture.

JOURNAL PROMPTS

◆ What gods and goddesses inspire me? Are there any I feel called to work with?

◆ What parts of my life, or the life of my community, need help right now? Is there a deity whose wisdom could help me in this area?

◆ How would embracing polytheism change how I see the world? If I shift my perception from oneness and the universe to diversity and the cosmos, what changes?

◆ What parts of my life are missing divinity and a connection with divine forces? Are there any?

◆ What myths, stories, and legends inspire me? Are there ways I can bring that wisdom into my life?

GUIDED MEDITATION

We talked in chapter 2 about how meditation is an essential tool in magic. Meditation isn't just a way to gain focus for working spells or a means to calm us down, though. It is also a great tool for connecting with spirits, deities, and ancestors. This is usually called *journeying* or, more colloquially, *guided meditation*.

Maybe you already have a deity you work with, or even several. If you do, you might not need this technique. If, however, you are feeling called in some of the ways we talked about to explore this type of relationship, then the following meditation might help.

What you'll need:

For meditation and journeying, the only thing you really need is yourself. Sometimes, though, sounds, smells, and physical sensations can help us get into the right headspace faster and more easily. Additionally, if you are trying to summon a specific deity or spirit, then burning incense, candles, or leaving offerings to them is usually a good idea.

+ Incense. If you are trying to summon a particular deity, I recommend burning herbs or resins that are associated with them.

+ A steady sound or rhythm. This is not for everyone, but I find steady, repetitive sounds can help me get into a meditative state much more easily. Many meditation apps have background noises you can use, or you can try searching for steady drumbeats on places like YouTube.

+ A quiet space

+ 10–20 minutes of free time

+ A glass of water, or another simple offering like a slice of bread. Again, this is not strictly necessary, but if you are essentially inviting someone over to your house, it's nice to offer them something to eat or drink.

The following meditation is written for those of you who want to start deity work, but don't have a clue whom to work with or where to start. If you do have an idea of whom you want to work with or who wants to work with you, you can easily amend the meditation below to be more specific.

At a time when you know you'll be alone and undisturbed, find a space to sit or lay down comfortably. Light your incense, play your sounds, leave out any offerings you might be presenting in front of you or on your altar. Do what you need to get relaxed.

Return to the breathing technique we went over in chapter 2, and breath steadily for about a minute. Set your intention for this meditation, and if you are looking to connect with a specific entity or pantheon, perhaps call out to them or say their name.

Eventually, once you have begun meditating, envision that you are sitting in a big, open field on the side of a hill. The grass is green, the sky is blue, and there is a gentle, warm breeze.

Far in the distance, something catches your attention. You stand up and begin to walk toward it. As you walk, take in your surroundings. What kind of plants are around you? Are there any buildings? Are you walking on a path of some sort? Try to simply observe whatever imagery comes up for you without expectation or judgment.

Slowly, the thing that caught your eye begins to come into focus. You see what you know is a temple at the end of a path and walk up to it. You know that this temple is home to a particular deity, but you aren't sure who just yet. Again, this temple might look any way at all—ancient, modern, rustic, or fancy. Accept whatever comes to you.

Begin to walk the grounds of the temple and take note of what it looks like. What plants are growing there? Are there symbols or artwork anywhere? Are other people here or are you alone? Does this place remind you of anything or anyone from myth, and do any names or figures approach you while you are here?

Now, this part is important. If the deity whose temple this is approaches you and asks to work with you, or asks something of you, request an obvious sign within the next week. If they agree, thank them.

When you are ready to leave, walk out of the temple the way you came. Walk slowly down the path that brought you there and feel the warm light of the sun grow brighter and brighter until your vision goes white.

Slowly return to your body. Without rushing yourself, stretch your arms and legs, take a deep breath, and sit or stand up. I recommend having a glass of water or something small to eat like crackers or fruit to ground you back in your body when you are done. Write down whatever symbols you saw, things you heard, or anything that stuck out to you as important.

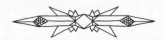

This temple exercise is a great way to communicate with and work with gods, goddesses, and other deities that you want to foster a deeper relationship with. You can come back to this place whenever you need to gain insight, ask questions, leave offerings, or simply *vibe*.

Now, why did I ask you to ask the deity to give you a sign in a week? There are a few reasons for this. One is that spirits are tricky, and you don't want to go around believing any- and everything they say. Sure, maybe this being is calling themself Apollo, but don't you want to be sure that's not just your brain or a spirit disguising themselves as Apollo?

The second is that once you start doing magic for a while, you'll realize gods fly in and out of your life just like neighbors you don't really know or birds you can sort of identify. If they really want to be your ally, then they should show you that. Remember, all relationships are two-way streets and this includes divine relationships.

So what is an obvious sign? Well, that's going to be a little bit up to you to determine. I would go back and look over the section on synchronicity (see page 34) and see if anything like that starts to happen. Maybe this being's symbol is an apple and your coworker brings in a bunch of apples to share the next day. Maybe their symbol is an oak tree and you get hit on the head by acorns several times that week. When in doubt, use divination to help straighten things out.

If no sign appears or things don't go how you'd like, don't worry. In my opinion, it's much better to figure out if a spark is there early on than to waste your time and money going down a path that isn't going to be fulfilling. If you are set on working with this deity, maybe you just need to do more research or show your seriousness in other ways. Try to remember not to get discouraged early on if things take work—like I said, all relationships do.

FURTHER READING

The Druid's Primer, Luke Eastwood
While this book focuses on druids and Celtic paganism, the way it approaches this path and the workings it gives would be a great introduction to many forms of paganism. With lists of deities, holidays, tools, and meditations on cosmology, I highly recommend this book to people interested in druidry or reconstructionist paganism.

The Pagan Book of Living and Dying, Starhawk
The road gets tough sometimes, and spirituality can be a powerful force to get us through those times. If you are more of an eclectic pagan and are looking for poems, rituals, and rites to guide you through life, Starhawk speaks with a powerful voice that can guide your way.

True to the Earth: Pagan Political Theology, Kadmus
If you're interested in not just going through the motions of ritual, but really letting paganism shape how you see the world, I highly recommend checking this book out. It's a book of philosophy that asks us to truly imagine an animist, pagan worldview—but let that excite you rather than scare you. It's short, easy to read, and not at all intimidating.

CHAPTER

8

WHERE TO GO FROM HERE

n his landmark book *Apocalyptic Witchcraft,* Peter Grey writes "Witchcraft does not mistake myths for history, it harnesses them to transform the future." As we reach the end of this book, I hope you know the value of history, as well as myth.

Look, we're talking about *magic* here. I want history and research to inform your spirituality, not make it boring or a chore. I don't know anyone whose practice is a 100 percent accurate reproduction of any ancient thing, not just because that isn't really possible, but also because magic is about actually connecting and conversing with the living cosmos, not having a scripted dialogue with it. I do silly things in my personal practice that have no basis at all in history—or quite frankly logic—but they work for me. As you grow, you will no doubt pick up some silly habits of your own.

My hope is that this book gives you the background and tools to decide what direction you want to head in and a little guidance as you start moving. What I don't want to do is suck all the magic out of magic. One phrase that gets used in magic a lot is "the map is not the territory." What I've hopefully done here is give you a map, but you have to travel it yourself. I'm sure you'll find things come up that you weren't prepared for or that we didn't cover. That's okay—that means you're actually getting somewhere!

With all that said, though, I can't help but give you a bit more advice on how to keep studying magic. In this final chapter I'm going to leave you with some research tips, ways to discern between sources, and advice for starting your own magical practice.

CREATING YOUR OWN PRACTICE

One of the good and terrifying things about magic is that it makes you take responsibility for your own spiritual practice and asks you to blaze your own path, at least to a certain extent. Unless you initiate into a tradition or join a formal religion, it's likely you'll have to start from scratch on pretty much everything—from holidays to daily practices to what to call yourself. This can be exciting at times and daunting at others. I'm not a guru, priestess, or leader in any sort of tradition. I'm also not interested in giving you a template or cookie-cutter practice to start with, but I have been doing this for a while so I've got a few tips for how to go from here.

SYSTEMS WILL NATURALLY COMPLICATE THEMSELVES

One thing I have learned over the years—after starting, stopping, and reforming my magical practice several times—is that you don't have to start off with complexity. It's actually much better to begin simply and get more complex. In fact, this complexity will form naturally over time. You might start meditating once a day with just a timer on your phone, then maybe you add music or incense to this practice. As you grow and explore, maybe you use planetary sounds or incense to match the day you are meditating. Maybe you meditate on specific spiritual writings or figures over long periods of time. Maybe from there, you naturally need to set up an altar where all your associated items are stored.

To an outsider, what you have set up is quite complicated, but it started as something very simple. The thing is, humans are programmed to look at change with suspicion, and changes in our daily routine are very difficult to make stick. If you try to start a new practice by acting like someone who has been doing this for years, you are going to fail, get frustrated, and give up. I know the urge to look cool and have a million books, candles, crystals, and animal skulls is a strong one, especially in an age of social media, but in my opinion, it really is best to start small and let things naturally grow more complicated.

COMPASSION FOR YOURSELF AND OTHER SEEKERS

It's very, *very* easy to look down on other magical people who you think are sillier, dumber, or worse at magic than you are. Believe me, I've had to hold myself back several times while writing this book. However, while we all like to have our fun at the expense of Priestess Willowbark MoonDragon or Frater Ichabod, we're ulti-mately all just students in the weirdest club on earth. I know magic is cool now, but it wasn't always this way, and I suspect there might be a time in the future when it goes back to being a nerdy thing once more. Try to be nice to people who are now where you once were or people who just got a bunch of bad information.

In addition, please be nice to yourself. It can be so easy to fall into the trap of thinking everyone else is a powerful sorcerer and you're just sitting in your room lighting candles. I have two published books on this subject, and I still feel that way sometimes. While being self-critical can be important to keep us hum-ble and refine our skills, try not to compare yourself to what you think others are doing or thinking. I promise you: everyone feels like they are doing this stuff "wrong" much of the time, but if what you are doing works for you and makes your life better, that's really all you have to worry about.

OLDER ≠ BETTER

It can sometimes feel like you need everything in your own practice to come from an ancient, preferably pre-Christian source. For whatever reason, people often associate ancientness with authenticity and modernity with fakery in magic. Even if you say you don't, this feeling can be very intrusive.

Some of this, I think, is understandable. Remember when we talked about Wicca and how, quite frankly, silly a lot of modern iterations of it got? I think a lot of people reacted to that by diving into history books and pulling out ideas and practices that came before the twentieth or nineteenth centuries as a way of finding shelter from a sea of crushed velvet and patchouli. Heck, I myself went this route. It should be obvious by now that I think historical context can only help your magical practice and that it's important to know where you are getting your information from. At the same time, I don't want this to lead anyone to a reactionary worship of the past.

People in the past often believed things that were bad, cruel, or flat-out wrong. The same way I wouldn't encourage you to rub belladonna on your eyelids or ask a father how much his eldest daughter's dowry is, I would not say that just because a magical practice or idea is old, it is good or worth doing. In the grimoire chapter, we went over the fact that these books were written by old monks with a lot of time on their hands, which means we must occasionally adapt what they wrote for modern people. Trying to stay true to source material is admirable, but I also think that through respectful adaptation we can often learn insights into the true heart of these practices.

You will also inevitably pick up things that arrive from modern sources or come up with your own tricks that work for you but have no historical precedent. So long as you aren't trying to pass off your Pokémon-card fortune-telling for an ancient Sumerian ritual, then this is more than fine.

JUST GO FOR IT

My goal with this book was to demystify the mystical and make magic accessible for you to get started, but I understand that you might still feel overwhelmed—maybe even more so than before. People don't want to be rude, fake, or reckless by doing the "wrong" thing most of the time, and I think this is a good impulse. It's good to have respect for magic and those who have been practicing it for a long time. It's smart to want safety and security while doing some pretty spooky things. All that said, though, at a certain point you have to put your books down and just do magic.

When I first started teaching myself how to cook, I was very precise with measurements, ingredients, and time. I followed instruction videos to the letter, and if I didn't have an ingredient on hand, I didn't make the thing. At the time, this was probably the right thing to do! I had no idea how to cook, and I was still getting the hang of it all. Now? I usually look at a picture of a meal and can figure out how to make it—if I'm really stuck, *maybe* I look at the ingredients list. The lesson here is that you get better at stuff you actually do. Imagine if I had just read cookbooks and never even tried a recipe out! I'd still be heating up frozen dinners every night and calling it cooking.

There will also, inevitably, be that voice in your head that says you aren't "good enough" or doing it "right." You know the best way to get rid of that voice? I hate to say it, but the answer is actually doing magic. I guarantee you, the more you do, the more successes you will have, and when you have fairly frequent proof that magic is real, it can go a long way toward quieting that voice. You aren't going to get it all "right" the first time, and you'll have many bad meals along the way, but what matters is trying stuff out and seeing what happens.

FURTHER RESEARCH

This might be your first book on magic, but if it is, I hope it won't be your last. There are more resources available to magical practitioners now than ever before—from books to blogs to videos. We have never been so rich in rabbit holes.

But with a wealth of information comes a wealth of confusion. It can be hard to know which sources to trust, what information is good information, and how to study magic going forward. With all this in mind, I want to give you some final tools to help you sort through resources and continue your magical studies.

ASSESSING SOURCES

How much time you want to spend assessing your sources depends, I think, on what you are planning on doing with the information you find. Going back to chaos magic principles for a second, if the generic book of spells your aunt got you for your birthday in a bid to connect with you works wonderfully, then maybe you don't have to track down the author and cross-reference the sources they use.

However, sometimes people will make claims in magical books, blogs, and videos that are pretty consequential if true. Spirituality can be a tool for connecting with the cosmos and making you a better person, or it can be a way for misinformation and harm to spread. We talked already about how people make very bold claims about race when it comes to paganism and magic, and the same can be said for gender, morality, and sexuality. You always want to have your wits about you when researching or studying magic.

So, while you don't have to bust this out for every guided meditation or drum circle you attend, it's good to keep the following handy when doing research.

CARS METHOD

We're going to be looking at the CARS method of evaluating sources—assessing *credibility, accuracy, reasonableness,* and *support.* This method was developed by Dr. Robert Harris to help assess the credibility of resources, especially those found online.

Credibility

Who is the source you are reading and how credible are they? What you're trying to vet here is "how does this person know what they claim to know?" It's very easy online, especially with magic, for someone to look like they are very serious and know what they are talking about. With the right lighting and enough skulls anyone can look like an expert, but do they actually understand what they are talking about? Finding credible sources can seem like a game of guts and trusting your instincts, but there are some good questions to ask that can help reveal if a source is credible or not.

Do they practice the type of magic they are talking about, or have they done their research on it?

Do they have a degree specializing in this subject?

Can you see if they've spoken on podcasts, taught at conferences, written any books, or seem to be well regarded by other experts in the field?

Accuracy

Here we are trying to figure out how accurate the information you are getting is. This can be difficult if you don't have a background in a subject, but try the following to get you started.

When was this published or posted? A more recent source might have more up-to-date information than something published decades ago.

What sources is this person using? Do they seem to be going off pure vibes about the past, or are they using a history book?

Are the sources they are using accurate? If you have the time, look up the sources they are using and apply this same method there.

How many sources are they citing? You don't need a whole library's worth to be accurate, but they should ideally cite at least more than one source.

Does this person seem to have a bias? Everyone has a bias, but does their bias seem to cloud their judgment and make them leave out important information?

Reasonableness

When it comes to magic, this can be a little difficult to determine, and at a certain point you might just have to trust your gut. If you are reading a source written by someone who practices magic and isn't just a historian or scholar, then it's possible that they will bring up spiritual experiences of their own to back up some of their claims.

This isn't a problem in and of itself—I've done it myself in this book several times. What you want to have here is what is technically referred to as a *bullshit meter,* to separate someone saying, "Diana seems to like it when you leave these offerings," from someone saying, "I am the only priestess of Diana, and she wants you to join my group that's definitely not a cult."

Is this person making specific or broad claims? Usually, the broader a claim, the less reasonable it is.

Does what this person is claiming even sound possible? Again, with *magic* this is a little hard to determine, but given what we've gone over in this book, does someone claiming to be from an ancient line of Celtic priests sound reasonable to you?

If this person has an online persona, how do they act online? Do they seem to lash out at the slightest criticism and constantly embroil themselves in drama? Online is bad, often, and fights happen, but does it happen to an unreasonable degree with this person?

Support

Similar to accuracy, you want to see how this person is supporting the ideas they put out there. If the person is making a bold, new claim, that's great—if they are backing it up with good sources. Are they?

Is anyone else saying what this person is saying, especially anyone credible? Again, new ideas are great, but if the person is presenting theirs as a fact and not a theory, maybe don't lend it as much credence.

Are they using evidence to support their claim? This might seem like an obvious thing to ask about, but you would be surprised how many posts, videos, and articles online don't use any evidence.

If the person is using statistics or numbers to back up their claim, where did they get those numbers from, and how are they being presented? You'd be surprised how much you can hide with some tricky number work.

RED FLAGS IN MAGIC BOOKS AND SOURCES

Before we go through this list, I want to say that just because a source is silly or wrong, doesn't always mean it has no value. There are plenty of books out there on money magic, love magic, and so on that maybe aren't "accurate," and maybe don't have a ton of historical basis, but that I think are basically harmless. If they work for you, then that's all they really need to do.

However, when I'm buying a new book, checking out a video, or reading a blog, there are a few red flags and warning signs that I look out for. These don't necessarily mean this person is bad or that they need to be called out in some dramatic way, but it does mean you might be wasting time and money—and no one wants that.

Below are some phrases and words I look for when picking up a book, looking at someone's blog, or going through someone's videos or tweets. Keep in mind, these words aren't bad, but for whatever reason they seem to attract bad scholarship, delusional thinking, or outright grifters. These aren't words to avoid entirely, but rather should be looked at as invitations to examine the text more closely.

Celtic

The Celts were real, they existed, and they did some cool stuff while they were around. Looking at the bookshelf in some New Age sections of the bookstore, though, you get the sense that the Celts are the Wakandans for white people. A lot of modern mythology gets put on the Celts, and a lot of people claim they practice "Celtic magic" when . . . we don't know much about what that really means!

The thing is, much of what we know about Celtic history and spirituality was recorded by invading Romans or survived through fragmented folklore that was often the target of colonial or religious forces. Celts didn't record their histories on paper or stone, and because of this, we just don't know as much about the ancient Celts as we do about, say, the ancient Egyptians. What this means is that while we can get an idea of what these people believed and how they lived, we will probably never get a complete portrait.

This doesn't stop people from writing libraries' worth of books on Celtic religious practices, holidays, lifestyle, and morals. I want to make it very clear, if someone who isn't a historian or who doesn't cite multiple good historical sources claims that this ritual, this spell, or this belief is something that comes straight from the ancient Celts, they are almost certainly wrong. I've seen so many books talk about drawing a magical circle as part of Celtic magic, which as you now know is totally false since it comes from grimoire magic, which comes from the Mediterranean. You can absolutely incorporate a magical circle into a Celtic-*inspired* practice, but claiming it comes from them is just a lie.

If you are interested in Celtic myths, magic, and history, use the CARS method and read sources from historians, universities, and scholars before reading books written by modern-day practitioners of "Celtic magic." This goes for pretty much all ancient civilizations, but I notice this silliness especially from the Celtic side of the bookstore. One extra piece of advice I would give is to check out books by druids on or about druidry, since they seem to have a more robust sense of scholarship overall.

Goddess Stuff

We've been over this a bit in this book, but I just want to drive a point home here. Goddess "stuff" can get really thorny, really quickly. To keep it simple, check out if the book, blog, or video you are interacting with makes any sweeping claims about ancient pan-European goddess cults or talks about ancient people simply worshipping "the goddess." Goddess work is beautiful and transformative, and goddess archetypes and mysteries have existed in some form or another since the Stone Age. I'm not claiming that anyone writing books on or claiming to work with the divine feminine or a particular goddess is a fraud or wrong. On the contrary, there has been some amazing work and scholarship on this subject in the past few years. I'm just saying to check which historical sources they are using and to watch out for any references to Margaret Murray or people who source heavily from her.

A good rule of thumb is to not trust those who do cite Murray. Like the Celts, goddess cults existed, some were very widespread, and seeing correlations between some deities is fine, but people get, let's say "creative," with these facts. If an author is claiming to be the priestess of an ancient, unbroken goddess cult (a real thing I have seen), simply put the book down and walk away.

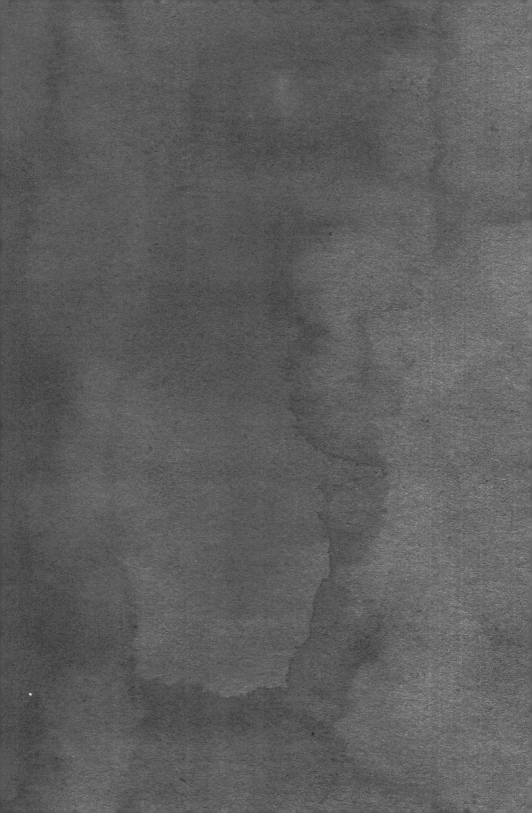

ACKNOWLEDGMENTS

A book like this is the result of a community of friends, colleagues, and found family that I am blessed to know and surround myself with. With that in mind, I need to thank the Diviners Brain Trust broadly, and a few people specifically.

Phil English, thank you for your help with the ceremonial magic chapter, and everything Thelema. 93.

Jess Lynch, thank you for all your help with the Kabbalah section, and Jewish mysticism as a whole.

Matthew Collura, thank you for notes, encouragement, and excitement for this book that kept me going.

Justin Wisner, thank you for all your amazing notes and suggestions in the grimoires chapter. Maybe I'll get a spell to summon Lucifer in the next book ;)

Autumn Whitehurst, you absolute ray of savage sunshine, thank you for uplifting me and helping me the whole way through this book.

Frank Sivili, thank you for unrelenting friendship and love.

To my editor, Shannon Fabricant, thank you for always believing in me and bringing out the best in my work.

To Allyson Kelley, your comments both challenged and soothed me in the best way possible. Thank you for helping this book stick to a high standard.

As always, I want to thank the trees on which this book is printed, and the workers who typeset, printed, bound, and transported it. Nothing would exist without you.

I want to thank my ancestors for carrying me here, and the gods that watch over me, specifically Babalon and Hekate, for blessing my work and carrying me over the finish line.

I also want to thank myself for not giving up, not giving in, and following my dreams like a true north star, even when it would have been easier to sink.

UM, SOURCES FOR THESE CLAIMS? OR SELECTED BIBLIOGRAPHY

Allen, Bartlett Capt. Robert. *Real Alchemy: A Primer of Practical Alchemy*. Hays (Nicolas) Ltd, U.S., 2009.

Carr-Gomm, Philip, and Richard Heygate. *The Book of English Magic*. London: Hodder & Stoughton Ltd., 2014.

Cave, Alfred A. *Indian shamans and English witches in seventeenth-century New England*. Salem, MA: Essex Institute Historical Collection, 1992.

Davies, Owen. *Grimoires: A History of Magic Books*. Oxford, England: Oxford University Press, 2010.

Federici, Silvia. *Caliban and the Witch: Women, the Body and Primitive Accumulation*. London: Penguin Books, 2021.

Flowers, Stephen E. *Icelandic Magic: Practical Secrets of the Northern Grimoires*. Rochester, VT: Inner Traditions, 2016.

Grey, Peter. *Apocalyptic Witchcraft*. London: Scarlet Imprint, 2013.

Harris, Robert. "Evaluating Internet Research Sources." *VirtualSalt,* June 26, 2001; http://www.virtualsalt.com/evalu8it.htm.

Hatsis, Thomas. *The Witches' Ointment: The Secret History of Psychedelic Magic*. Inner Traditions Bear and Comp, 2015.

Howe, Katherine. *The Penguin Book of Witches*. S.L.: Penguin, 2015.

Josselyn, John. *New-England's rarities discovered in birds, beasts, fishes, serpents, and plants of that country*. Boston: W. Veazie, 1865.

Lecouteux, Claude. *The Book of Grimoires: The Secret Grammar of Magic*. Rochester, VT: Inner Traditions, 2013.

Morgan, Lee. *A Deed Without a Name: Unearthing the Legacy of Traditional Witchcraft*. Moon Books, 2013.

Pearson, Nigel G. *Treading the Mill: Workings in Traditional Witchcraft*. London: Troy Books, rev. ed. 2017.

Place, Robert Michael, and Rosemary Guiley. *Magic and Alchemy*. New York: Chelsea House Publishers, 2009.

Porterfield, Charles. *A Deck of Spells: Hoodoo Playing Card Magic in Rootwork and Conjure*. Forestville, CA: Lucky Mojo Curio Company, 2015.

Russell, Jeffrey Burton. *Witchcraft in the Middle Ages*. London: Cornell University Press, 2004.

Sollée Kristen J. *Witches, Sluts, Feminists: Conjuring the Sex Positive*. Berkeley: ThreeL Media, 2017.

Starhawk. *The Spiral Dance: A Rebirth of the Ancient Religion of the Great Goddess*. San Francisco: HarperSanFrancisco, 1989.

Simpson, J. "Margaret Murray: Who Believed Her, and Why?" *Folklore* 105: 1–2, 89–96; https://www.tandfonline.com/doi/pdf/10.1080/0015587X.1994.9715877.

UK Parliament website. "Witchcraft." Accessed January 6, 2022; https://www.parliament.uk/about/living-heritage/transformingsociety/private-lives/religion/overview/witchcraft/.

Wachter, Aidan. *Six Ways: Approaches & Entries for Practical Magic*. Toronto: Red Temple Press, 2018.

Wilby, Emma. *The Visions of Isobel Gowdie: Magic, Witchcraft and Dark Shamanism in Seventeenth-Century Scotland*. Eastbourne, East Sussex: Sussex Academic Press, 2010.

FURTHER READING

AFRICAN DIASPORIC RELIGIONS

Orishas, Goddesses, and Voodoo Queens: The Divine Feminine in the African Religious Traditions, by Lilith Dorsey

Born of Blood and Fire, by Richard Ward

Exu & the Quimbanda of Night and Fire, by Nicholaj de Mattos Frisvold

Pomba Gira & the Quimbanda of Mbùmba Nzila, by Nicholaj de Mattos Frisvold

Palo Mayombe: The Garden of Blood and Bones, by Nicholaj de Mattos Frisvold

Cuban Santeria, by Raul Canizares

Haitian Vodou: An Introduction to Haiti's Indigenous Spiritual Traditions, by Mambo Chita Tann

CHAOS MAGIC

The Chaos Protocols, by Gordon White

Book of Lies: The Disinformation Guide to Magick and the Occult, Edited by Richard Metzger

Prime Chaos, by Phil Hine

GRIMOIRES AND SPELL BOOKS

An Excellent Booke of the Arte of Magicke, edited by Phil Legard, essays by Alexander Cummins, foreword by Dan Harms

The Book of Oberon, by Daniel Harms, James R. Clark & Joseph H. Peterson

The Wicked Shall Decay: Charms, Spells and Witchcraft of Old Britain, by A. D. Mercer

A Cunning Man's Grimoire, Edited by Dr. Stephen Skinner & David Rankine

CEREMONIAL MAGIC

The Magician's Workbook, by Steve Savedow

The Chicken Qabalah of Rabbi Lamed Ben Clifford, Lon Milo DuQuette

Magick in Theory and Practice, by Aleister Crowley

The Red Goddess, by Peter Grey

WITCHCRAFT

The British Book of Spells & Charms, Graham King

A Deed Without a Name, Lee Morgan

Treading the Mill, Nigel G. Pearson

Apocalyptic Witchcraft, Peter Grey

Mastering Witchcraft, Paul Huson

PAGANISM, GODS, AND GODDESSES

Being Pagan: A Guide to Re-Enchant Your Life, Rhyd Wildermuth

Asatru, by Erin Lale

The Orphic Hymns, translated by Patrick Dunn

The Oracles of Apollo: Practical Ancient Greek Divination for Today, by John Opsopaus

Norse Mythology, by John Lindow

Religion and Magic in Ancient Egypt, by Ann Rosalie David

INDEX